Don and Janice Schaeffer

The Australian Alternative

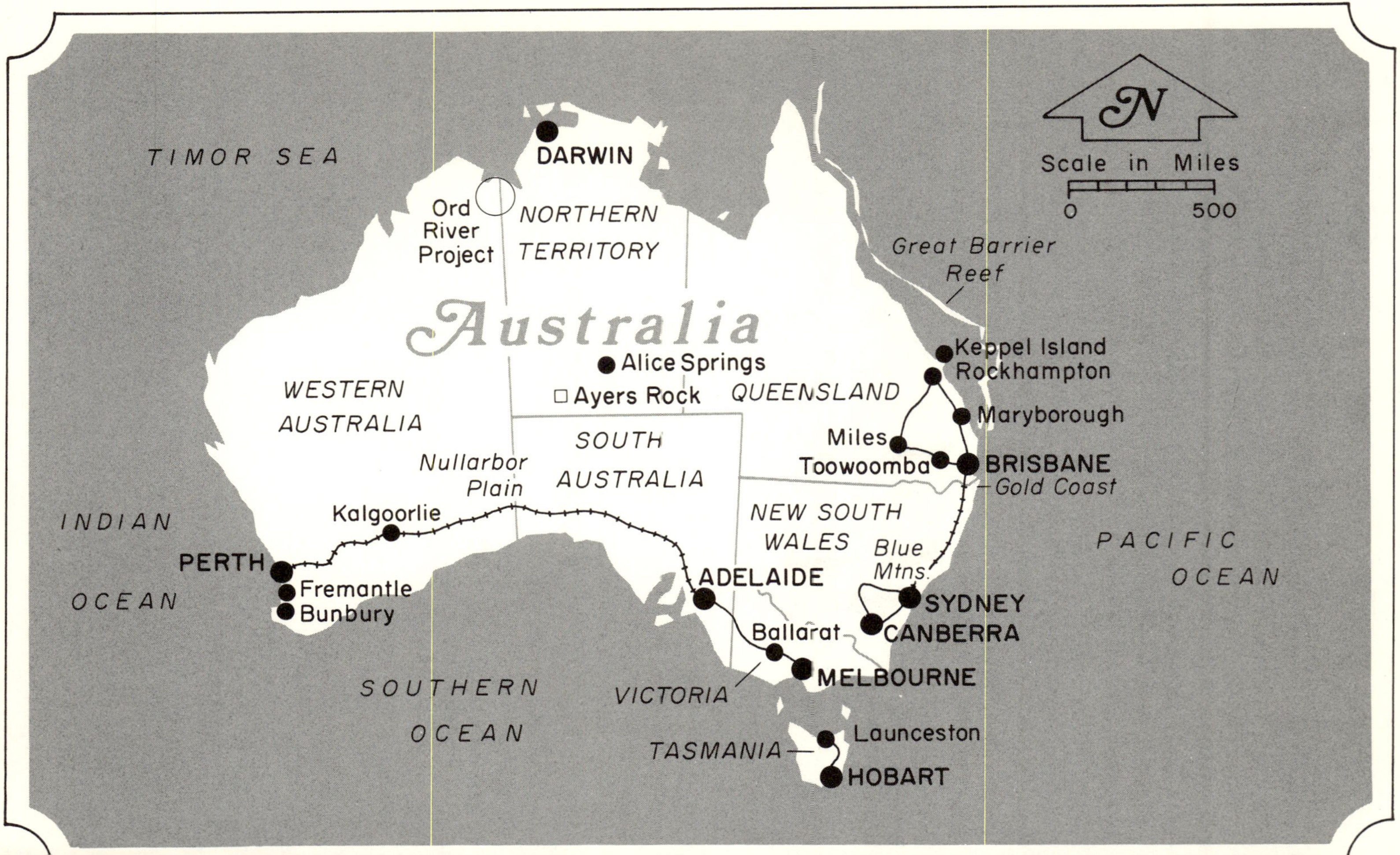

N
Scale in Miles
0
500
TIMOR SEA
DARWIN
Ord
River
Project
NORTHERN
TERRITORY
Great Barrier
Reef
Australia
Alice Springs
Ayers Rock
QUEENSLAND
WESTERN
AUSTRALIA
Keppel Island
Rockhampton
Maryborough
Miles
Toowoomba
BRISBANE
Gold Coast
SOUTH
AUSTRALIA
Nullarbor
Plain
NEW SOUTH
WALES
Blue
Mtns.
Kalgoorlie
INDIAN
OCEAN
PERTH
Fremantle
Bunbury
ADELAIDE
SYDNEY
CANBERRA
Ballarat
MELBOURNE
PACIFIC
OCEAN
SOUTHERN
OCEAN
VICTORIA
Launceston
TASMANIA
HOBART

The *Australian* Alternative

Laura E. & Odie B. Faulk

WITH NANCY M. & RICHARD D. FAULK

ARLINGTON HOUSE·PUBLISHERS
NEW ROCHELLE, NEW YORK

Copyright © 1975 by Arlington House

All rights reserved. No portion of this book may be reproduced without written permission from the publisher except by a reviewer who may quote brief passages in connection with a review.

Manufactured in the United States of America

Library of Congress Cataloging in Publication Data

Faulk, Laura E
   The Australian alternative.

   1. Australia—Description and travel—1951-
2. Faulk, Laura E. 3. Faulk, Odie B. I. Faulk,
Odie B. II. Title.
DU105.F28   919.4'04'6   75-6975
ISBN 0-87000-251-1

Contents

I. Introduction 9
II. Hawaii and Fiji 21
III. Tasmania 43
IV. Victoria and South Australia 77
V. Out West 105
VI. Sydney, Canberra, and the Outback 129
VII. The Northeast 155
VIII. The Australian Alternative in Retrospect 179

The *Australian* Alternative

I.
Introduction

AT ONE TIME or another a surprising number of Americans, probably even a majority of them, have thought about moving to a foreign country either for a short visit or even permanently. Most do so because of being seized by a temporary wanderlust, others because they want adventure, and yet others because of romantic visions of the different. However, a growing number of Americans are thinking of moving away from their country because they feel society here is deteriorating, that the nation is bound for perdition apace. Society indeed is in turmoil, for we apparently are at one of those transitional periods of sharp turning with the new directions not yet fully perceived—and definitely not appreciated by all.

The past decade has seen antiwar crusades where the flag of our nation's enemy was flaunted proudly at public gatherings. On the evening television news we have seen students shouting down in the name of freedom those with whom they disagreed; national guardsmen are shown firing into the ranks of collegians and killing four of them at Kent State University; and other young Americans have been interviewed to determine their reasons for fleeing to Canada to avoid induction into the country's armed forces. In 1972 one of the major political parties in the United States nominated for the presidency a man who had just returned from a meeting of the World Council of Churches wherein he had led in a movement to condemn this country. By a year and a half later both the president and the vice president, who won election by one of the largest margins in history, were gone, each having been forced to resign under extreme pressure. National politicians equally guilty of crimes of omission and commission had joined in the mad push to obtain the impeachment or the resignation of the president, and in the process had brought to office a chief executive who had not won the nomination of a major political party or secured a single popular vote from the public.

Simultaneously during this decade, our politicians have been telling the voters that busing our children to achieve some magic racial balance is like fried liver: it is good for us even if we do not like it, and we should swallow it without question or complaint. Moreover, this decade has seen our "intellectuals" telling us that the United States in the past has mistreated its native races, the blacks, the Latin Americans, and almost everyone else of any ethnic origin other than Anglo-Saxon. In short, Americans were being told that their country was and is guilty of every sin since the fall of Adam and Eve—and just possibly of that also.

Going hand in hand with this political and intellectual ferment has been a crime rate spiraling upward to an alarming degree, while our learned jurists have decreed that the criminal is the victim and society is the culprit. Labor leaders have called for pay increases not tied in any way to increases in productivity, and supine—if not sympathetic—bureaucrats have helped them with their demands by allowing strikers to collect free food stamps and unemployment compensation. And the national government has lived beyond its means, congressmen appropriating funds willy-nilly in the hope of buying reelection, and the national debt soaring toward the five-hundred-billion-dollar level. Inflation has resulted, a rampant, galloping inflation that eats away at savings and that has forced two humiliating devaluations of the American dollar. The stock market by late summer 1974 had fallen disastrously, new housing seemed the impossible dream to many working citizens, and our schools were unable to teach Johnny and Mary either to read or to do simple sums in arithmetic. All this transpires while our aspirants for the presidency in 1976 outdo one another in making political promises to the voters.

Little wonder then that many Americans are unhappy and restless. They know that the endless repetition of a lie does not make it true, for they know their children are exposed to drugs in schools that are teaching less every year; that there are professors of economics in colleges and universities who cannot balance a checkbook; and that too much of the nation is worshipping youth and ignoring wisdom.

These unhappy Americans look at the rest of the world to see if there is some place where sanity still holds sway, where politicians do not try to solve all problems by throwing money at them or by trying to legislate changes in human nature, where age and experience still count for more than callow youth, where the young are not demanding legal lotus leaves in the form of legislation authorizing the use of marijuana, and where truth is still regarded as something constant and not subject to individual interpretation. One of the countries that the restless American often singles out as perhaps suitable for immigration on a short- or long-term basis and as preferable to America is Australia. Political cartoonists have recognized this American infatuation with Australia as a potential home by showing, after each election in which a liberal wins, the conservative packing his suitcases while his wife asks, "But, dear, what will we do in Australia?"

The "Land Down Under" likewise attracts the attention

of the restless American looking for adventure. He reads that Australia is approximately the same size as the continental United States, yet contains only some 13,000,000 citizens. Here, then, is a place with elbowroom and wide-open spaces where a man yearning to breathe free can stretch. And, he reads, there are kangaroos and wild dogs and natives, and men in the "Outback" still wearing guns. This, he thinks, is a last frontier where he can test himself.

There are many other reasons for the interest in Australia. Some see it as a land of economic opportunity, for there is no capital-gains tax. Others are attracted to it because of the current wave of nostalgia sweeping the United States; they hear the common statement that Australia is thirty years behind America, and they want to return to the past. Still others want to escape the crowded American cities—to return to the land. And a few are recruited by the Australian government because they possess some skill needed in that country. Yes, many Americans have been enchanted by Australia. "After all," one person tells another, "Australia is the foreign nation most similar to the United States, and they speak English. You don't have to learn a foreign language, the cultural heritage is the same, and Americans are welcome. The two countries have been allies for years." Besides, the beaches are great, the beer is good, and the climate mild.

Like so many Americans, my wife and I for years have wanted to visit Australia. In 1958 we considered moving there so I could work on my master's degree, and almost a decade later I corresponded with one of the Australian state universities about my taking a teaching position there. However, one thing and another prevented our moving there either to study or to work. Mainly we hesitated because to make such a move involved a serious break in our lives. How could we continue to make house payments and car payments and all the other payments that every patriotic adult owes if we were nine thousand miles away? And Australian universities begin their academic year in late

January, finishing in early December. If I took a job there I would finish my year's work in December, but upon returning to the United States I would be without employment until the following September. And accepting a job there, one which would pay our passage over and back, meant agreeing to work there for two years. It meant selling our home and car, even our furniture, and moving nine thousand miles to a land we had never seen.

The nagging question in the backs of our minds was: What if we get down there and don't like it? This thought, no doubt, has occurred to almost every American who has considered moving there. Moreover, we wondered what the countryside would look like in Australia; to what could we compare it in the United States? Which of its cities would we prefer, or would we rather try for one of the suburban, even rural areas? We knew that similar questions about Australia had troubled other Americans, for we had seen many advertisements over the years offering "information booklets about Australia" for sale; these yet appear in many popular magazines.

In the summer of 1974 we decided to make this journey, for that is when I became eligible for a sabbatic leave from the university where I am employed. At this institution, as at most in the United States, professors are eligible to apply for a leave of absence with pay after they have worked six years. The seventh year (or sabbatical year) is to be used to undertake study or research that will make the faculty member more valuable to his institution—that is, he should learn something that will make him a better teacher or a more productive faculty member, or both.

For many years I have been teaching the history of the American West, while my research interest has been concentrated on the American Southwest. Therefore, I wanted to make a comparative study of the influence of the frontier in Australia and of that in the United States, especially the influence of aridity on the techniques of mining, farming, and ranching. However, most of the research I did and the information I collected in connection with this project are omitted from these pages; occasionally my studies in this area do intrude where they seem to offer some insights into Australia and its people.

When to our great joy the administrators at my university approved my sabbatic leave, my family and I decided to keep detailed journals of our travel. We believed that we were typical of many Americans unhappy with the mood and direction of the 1970s, but that we were sufficiently happy with the United States not to want to move precipitously. We believed that what we would see, find, think, and experience might be of benefit or of insight to other Americans who feel the same way and who might be contemplating a move to Australia.

In the writing of this book, the word *we* appears frequently and refers to the four of us: father, mother, son, and daughter —the typical American family so often portrayed in commercials on television. Yet obviously a book cannot be authored by four people, for writing is a solitary venture. Therefore, while this book carries the byline of both mother and father—and acknowledges the contributions of our children— I, the father, inherited the task because of past efforts to write history and because I had minored in English in college. However, because of the authority conferred on her by virtue of her experience and marital status, to say nothing of her sex, my wife reserved to herself the right to blue-pencil the copy and to shape the final product by comment and suggestion as it proceeded from draft to draft. And our children were consulted for opinions and suggestions during this same process, so that the result is a joint effort.

Years ago I took a course in the history of the British Commonwealth. Other than this I had no special qualifications for writing about Australia. The *I* used throughout the book is a Texan by birth and Southwesterner by inclination who this summer (1974) attained his forty-first birthday. I hold the usual academic degrees possessed by a professor of history. In years past I have been in the U.S. Marine Corps for five and one-half years, worked as a roustabout in the oil fields, loaded Coca-Cola trucks, labored as a short-order cook, and even worked as a carpenter's apprentice. In addition, I have taught two years at the seventh-grade level and a decade and more at such institutions as Texas A. & M. and the University of Arizona. Presently I am professor and head of the Department of History at Oklahoma State University, find my hairline receding, and vote the Republican ticket. Laura is younger than I am—although when we have a "discussion," I threaten to tell the neighborhood wives that I do not mind being married to an older woman, a story they naturally would choose to believe in preference to the obvious truth. Laura holds a bachelor's degree in accounting, but since our marriage has devoted herself to the harder task of making a home for us and our two children rather than seeking some career goal. She is the practical one in our household, and to her fell the unhappy task of keeping the account of our expenses so that we would not have to declare bankruptcy upon our return.

Richard, our redheaded son, passed his thirteenth birthday on March 6 (a date I remember because this was the day in 1836 when the Alamo fell to invading Mexicans). By stages he has aspired to become a professional baseball player, a professional golfer, an architect, a raiser of race horses, and a dentist; however, yesterday's "definitely" is tomorrow's "maybe"—meanwhile life is fun. He plays little-league baseball, rides horseback, and almost beats me at golf. Nancy, our daughter, turned eleven this summer on August 15. She is not as easygoing as Richard, experiencing greater extremes of emotions. Brown-haired and blue-eyed, she wants to own a ranch in Arizona and there raise horses, but she also wants a summer home in Vermont to escape the heat. Until that time she will likely continue playing the piano, practicing her ballet, riding horseback, rearranging the furniture in her room, and collecting stuffed animals. I can say with total impartiality and extreme candor that I am prejudiced about my children. I think they are great.

Actually we began preparing for this trip years ago by vacationing all over the United States. Since 1965, when Richard was four and Nancy two, we had visited forty-seven of the fifty states, missing only Hawaii, Alaska, and North Dakota. Hawaii we would see on this vacation; Alaska is a promise we have made ourselves for the future; and North Dakota—well, we have told the children that we will pass that up because they need something to look forward to when they are grown. But our travels have made us appreciative of the United States and sharpened our eye for geographic variations.

Last Christmas we began more specific preparations by giving one another new luggage as presents. Our old suitcases were so battered as to be useless; in fact, we did not even bother to put them into the attic "for future use." Then came the paperwork necessary for our passport, something we had never before needed. I had been to Japan and Korea in 1951-52 and to Japan and Okinawa in 1954-55, courtesy of the Marine Corps, and as a family we had gone to Canada and Mexico; but neither of us had applied for a passport before. In truth, neither of us had ever even seen one. We learned that we could get separate ones at ten dollars apiece, or else we could get one for the family for ten dollars. That was an easy decision, for passports have a lifespan of five years and our children would not be grown by then. Getting our passport photographs reminded us that we also needed a family portrait (no doubt photographers pick up a good bit of business that way), and then we went to the post office to have our passport forms filled out. For a fee of two dollars this was done, and ten days later our passport came in the mail. All in all, it was a simple affair.

Next we went to a local travel agent to get tickets and help with our visa. Our plans were to spend a week in Hawaii and a couple of days in Fiji before reaching Australia.

And, inasmuch as we were leaving late in May, we would be arriving just at the onset of winter in Australia; therefore, we determined to go directly to Tasmania, the island state to the south of the Australian continent and the part where winter would hit the hardest. Thus we wanted roundtrip tickets from Oklahoma City to Sydney and tickets from Sydney to Launceston, Tasmania; our return tickets we left with no confirmed date, for that we would decide while we were in Australia. In short order our travel agent had us booked for a flight from Oklahoma City to Dallas, then from Dallas to Honolulu aboard a Braniff International 747; after touring Hawaii, we would fly on Canadian Pacific Airlines to Nadi, Fiji, stay at the Dominion Hotel for two days, and then proceed to Sydney aboard Qantas, the Australian airline. From Sydney to Launceston we would be aboard Trans-Australian Airlines (TAA), one of the two major domestic airlines in that country.

As I said, securing these tickets posed no problem—except paying for them. We learned that on international flights there are no family rates as there are on domestic flights within the United States. And inasmuch as Richard was thirteen years of age, the airlines regarded him as an adult—and subject to paying an adult fare. Therefore, we had to pay for three and one-half tickets roundtrip from Oklahoma City to Sydney and one-way from Sydney to Launceston, a total of some $5,600. (However, if we had been intending to stay less than thirty-five days, we could have flown from Los Angeles to Sydney and returned for about $3,000, and this would have included two weeks' lodging at first-class motels and a rental car for two weeks with five hundred free miles. But because we intended to stay for three months, we had to pay the full fare. And the fare I quoted above was economy class, not first class.)

Getting an Australian visa proved more difficult. We had to fill out its forms, a simple procedure, and mail them and a photograph, along with our passport, to the Australian consulate in Los Angeles; and with these we had to send a letter from our travel agent certifying that we had roundtrip tickets that would bring us back to the United States. These procedures, of course, are to ensure that American tourists are not stranded in Australia without a ticket home, and just possibly to keep certain races out of that country. Two weeks later our passport returned, and in it was our visa; this stated that we were eligible to enter Australia an unlimited number of times in the next five years. We also were told in blunt English that we were not to take employment while visiting the country, nor were we to attempt to enroll for study at any Australian institution of higher learning. (Securing a visa to study or to work, as well as to immigrate, takes about three months, and the applicant bears the responsibility of proving that he is someone the Australian government feels would be welcome in that country. Australian officials know that their country is not suitable for everyone, and they deliberately try to discourage those who try to immigrate. Moreover, thus far they have refused entry permits to political undesirables, political malcontents, and certain racial groups.)

Along with our passport and visa, the Australian consulate also sent us a packet of tourist information about the country. Included in this were *Australia Travellers' Guide, Australia Welcomes You,* and *Australia Facts and Figures,* all of which are self-explanatory. In addition, there were *Karinya,* a title which was taken from the aboriginal word meaning "happy home" or "peaceful country," and which was a slick picture magazine from the Australian News and Information Bureau; *The Sydney Opera House,* also very slick and professional, and supplied courtesy of the Australian Information Service; and a few small items such as *Australia's Great Outback,* which apparently is designed to lure the traveler yet deeper into the country. This same packet, along with that supplied free to prospective immigrants, both of which can be had free of charge from any Australian consulate, is what you get for an average of two dollars if you answer some of those magazine advertisements offering information to those interested in Australia.

Finally, as we prepared to leave, we sought information about the health requirements for entering Fiji and Australia, along with the other countries we thought we might visit on our return home: New Zealand and Samoa. We were assured that nothing was needed, not even a smallpox vaccination. Our travel agent consulted all her books and bulletins and assured us that we needed nothing. So also were we told by our county health service, which studied the relevant government documents. Likewise we were assured by our doctor's office that no shots or vaccinations were required. We would be allowed into Fiji without question, for the United States was not regarded as an infected area. And the Australian government would not stop us from entering there even if we stayed two days in Fiji, while the New Zealanders would not require any shots if we entered their country by way of Australia. Nor would American authorities bother us as we came home (for we intended to visit only American Samoa). In short, everyone and every document assured us that we did not need to carry an international immunization card certifying that we had received certain shots or vaccinations.

"Besides," we told ourselves after these assurances, "the worst that can happen to us is that somewhere along the line we might have to take a smallpox vaccination. Those can't be any worse there than here, and we will not be quarantined." Thus happy to avoid taking any shots, we did nothing. Little did we dream of the trouble this decision would cause us as the trip proceeded—to say nothing of the cost, for we could have had them at our county health center for just fifty cents apiece.

The day before we departed I made one final resolution. I decided to quit smoking. I had started this habit when I was sixteen, at which age I joined the Marine Corps. Five years later I quit the habit, and I stayed off it for five and one-half years, only to begin again. For the past six years I had smoked only a pipe, believing that this was healthier than cigarettes, but much as I enjoyed the habit I wanted to quit. And what better time, I reasoned, than during a trip such as this; our travels would be a definite change of routine, and I hoped the distractions of the trip would make quitting much easier. Thus on the evening before we left home I gave my pipes to my children; they showed their distaste for the smell of the smoke I had been blowing out by taking a hammer to my "adult pacifiers."

The next morning we were off, leaving the keys to our house with neighbors and commending our yard to the care of a trustworthy college lad in the vicinity. A friend drove us to the airport in Oklahoma City. Our suitcases were heavy and our travel bags were stuffed with unused film, while in our pockets we each carried a blank journal waiting to be filled with our impressions. The story that follows is taken almost literally from the notes we jotted, but to these I have added background information on some of the cities and places we visited. We have no illusions that we are great authorities on Australia, nor do we posture ourselves as experts. Rather, what follow are our observations and our comments—plus a few of our prejudices and biases and opinions. We believe these will be of interest to anyone thinking of going to Australia for a short or a long visit; we hope they will be even more than interesting—perhaps even useful.

II.

Hawaii and Fiji

UNTIL THIS SUMMER of 1974, with its energy crunch and fifty-five-mile-per-hour speed limit, the seventy-mile drive from our home in Stillwater to the airport in Oklahoma City took about an hour and five minutes. Now it takes about an hour and a half. Yet the flight from Oklahoma City to Dallas, a distance of about two hundred miles, requires only twenty-five minutes on a passenger jet. Figures such as these always drive home to me how air travel has revolutionized our concepts of distance. When we lived in Tucson, it took us thirty-five minutes to drive from our home on the north side of town to the airport, but only thirty-two minutes to fly from Tucson to El Paso.

Arriving at the new Dallas-Fort Worth International Airport, we had three hours to wait, so we used the time to ride around this seventeen-thousand-acre monstrosity and look at it closely. Someone once told me that he believed when he died and departed for the hereafter, no matter which direction he traveled, he would have to change planes in

Dallas. Such is the regional significance of this airport. And it does seem that no matter where I go from Oklahoma, I have to go first to Dallas. At least this new airport is more modern than the old Love Field in Dallas, but it sprawls so that someone changing planes here needs lots of time—and a pocketful of change. The bus between the various terminals costs a quarter as does a local telephone call, and the machines that make change give only ninety-five cents for a dollar bill.

This first part of our trip, despite our first glimpse of the new Dallas-Fort Worth airport, was no particular thrill for any of the four of us, for we all had flown many times. However, we were very excited about the next part. We had asked our travel agent to book some part of our flight on a Boeing 747; none of us had ever been on one, and we had been reading that several airlines were grounding 747s until passenger traffic increased and the fuel crisis ended. Our agent had found that Braniff International had a direct flight every day from Dallas to Honolulu; it departed at 1:00 P.M. and arrived in Hawaii at 3:45 P.M. local time—after gaining five hours through flying westward.

Even before we saw this giant, we realized how big it was because of the size of the waiting room for the flight. The airline keeps an Aloha Room adjacent to the normal boarding area, and in this it serves free soft drinks and coffee —and tries to convey a festive, holiday mood. A flight such as this is not one used by normal airline customers; rather it is almost wholly a vacationers flight, and the airline wants to participate in the illusion of glamour, romance, and fun, all of which the state of Hawaii packages so wonderfully.

Once aboard the 747 and in our seats in the area designated for nonsmokers, we looked around—and found the airplane measured up to our expectations. It is almost as big as the television commercials make it appear. However, back in the economy section we were not standing around a piano bar or getting free golf lessons from Arnold Palmer. Most of the people on the plane, it quickly became apparent, were on a group tour and knew one another. They were drinking so heavily that the stewardesses were little more than flying bartenders; these passengers stood in the aisles laughing and talking, taking pictures with their pocket cameras, and smoking like chimneys. I am always amazed at how silly some people can act when they get away from home on a vacation, especially on a tour; apparently they feel they are paying so much for fun that they *should* have fun, and so they go about it with a kind of grim determination.

I was not missing my pipe particularly, for in the normal process of breathing I was inhaling as much if not more nicotine than I usually got from my pipe. (And few people realize how offensive a cigarette is to a pipe smoker; the nonsmoker might assume that tobacco is all the same, but it is not.) I began wondering if my smoking had ever been as offensive to others as this was proving to be to me; I consoled myself with the thought that my pipe was not as bad as cigarettes and that six years earlier, when I smoked cigarettes, these were so commonly used that I offended very few people.

The stewardesses at last cleared the drinkers-smokers out of the aisles and served lunch, after which they turned into ticket sellers for a movie. Then came sandwiches and soft drinks. But this entertainment and dining could not keep my posterior from growing numb; sitting there for seven hours and forty-five minutes grew tiresome. When at last we landed at Honolulu, it should have been 8:45 P.M., but the stewardesses assured us that it was only 3:45. For the first time I really began to understand what *jet lag* meant. At home—where "real time" prevailed—it was dark, and civilized people were sitting down for a couple of hours of television or reading before going to bed. Yet here the local citizens had not even gone home from work.

We were greeted by an agent of the tour company that was to show us the islands in this paradise of the Pacific, and she gave each of us a lei of genuine flowers. The pictures in the brochure about our tour (and in almost all the others about Hawaii) showed the newcomer getting his lei from a beautiful native girl—and the one giving us ours was fairly attractive—but the brochure did not say how ridiculous and conspicuous this makes a newcomer feel. I suspect that everyone arriving in Hawaii and having a string of flowers draped about his neck feels silly.

We then proceeded down to the baggage area to recover our luggage, a process that always amazes and relieves me. When you check into an airport, your luggage is placed on a conveyor belt to be swallowed by the mouth at the nearest wall; then, at your destination, your luggage is regurgitated from some other mouth. At least, such is the theory. This time, on this first stop of the biggest vacation of our lives, the system naturally failed to operate. We were subjected to the ultimate indignation and frustration of our computerized and mechanized world: lost baggage. Prior to our departure our travel agent had given us special tags which the tour operator specified we were to place on our suitcases. Little did we or our travel agent know—or, apparently, did the tour operator care—that all those people on our airplane who were traveling together on a package trip were given the exact same tags for their luggage so it could be kept together. Thus our luggage was taken off with theirs before the rest of it came up to the baggage claim area at the Honolulu airport. The Braniff agent assured us that he would do everything possible to locate our luggage, and reluctantly we departed for our hotel.

We were driven into town in a tour limousine crowded if not with luggage at least with people. And the driver looked as though he had some native Hawaiian blood. During the remainder of our stay on the island, we noted that every business connected with the tourist trade tried to have native Hawaiians visible; this was true at restaurants, hotels, and souvenir stands as well as on boats, buses, and in limousines.

Arriving at our hotel reminded us firsthand how local

merchants were gouging the mainlanders. By city ordinance in Honolulu it is illegal for more than three persons to stay in one hotel room; thus we had to rent two rooms in our Waikiki hotel at a cost of well over fifty dollars a day. Nor could we rush out to enjoy the surf and swim in the Pacific; we could not even paddle about in the fresh water of the swimming pool. Our swimming suits were in our suitcases. With nothing else to do, we had dinner in the hotel, looked at the overpriced Hawaiian shirts and muu-muu dresses, which every tourist is expected to purchase, and went to bed. That evening at 9:30, after we had been asleep for almost two hours (for it was 2:30 A.M. at home), a Braniff employee called to say that he had located five of our six suitcases and that these would be sent up to our room shortly.

The next morning, Sunday, we awakened at 4:30, an hour which no doubt would seem ridiculous to a Hawaiian but which was late for us, according to our internal clocks. During the remainder of our stay in Hawaii, I noticed that tourists regularly would begin strolling the sidewalks in Waikiki looking for somewhere to get a cup of coffee; for them the hour was late morning, but in Honolulu nothing was open.

That Sunday morning, however, we were interested more in finding our missing suitcase than in getting a cup of coffee. In fact, I was sufficiently wrought up not even to think of wanting to smoke. The previous evening the Braniff baggage agent had told me that he had found our five bags at the Hilton Hawaiian Village. Therefore I called the number listed in the yellow pages for this establishment to see if our other suitcase had been found there. The bell captain at the Hilton Hawaiian Village proved surly, but at last he told me that our other suitcase indeed was there. I asked him to send it to us by cab, to which he reluctantly agreed (for he would get no tip this way). I hung up the telephone wishing that Mr. Hilton would pay less attention to his love life and more toward improving the attitude of his employees.

25

Our dinner the evening before was bad—and matched the food served us this morning. Except for the very, very expensive restaurants at the tourist hotels in Hawaii, we found the food uniformly bad, and we are not gourmets. I believe these hotels deliberately served wretched food in their less-expensive restaurants to force the tourists to dine in the more-expensive places. There are two categories of restaurants at the hotels along Waikiki Beach: the outrageously expensive ones with good food, and those with outrageously terrible food at prices that would be deemed first class in nontourist places. Unless you have a thick wallet, it takes the stomach of a water buffalo or of an eighteen- or twenty-year-old to survive. And Hawaii seems to be filled with eighteen- to twenty-year-old kids searching for their identity while spending their parents' money, along with middle- and old-aged couples looking for some romanticized paradise as they apply suntan lotion and peel away sunburned skin. Those people in the latter category are the victims of ad writers for travel agents. They have seen too many postcards saying, "Wish you were here."

This morning we were off to the island of Kauai on our tour, a self-pacing one for which we had been given a book of coupons. At 7:30 we boarded a Hawaiian Airlines DC-9 for the brief flight from one island to the next. From the window of this plane the blue surf of the Pacific and the verdure of the mountains looked just like the slick photographs in the tourist literature. They truly were magnificent—and almost made me think that the cost was worthwhile. Once on Kauai, however, we returned to the reality of crowds of tourists. We were jammed on a bus and taken to see the "sights": the Grand Canyon of the Pacific, Fern Grotto, the Blowhole, a boatride on the Wailua River, even the cottage used in filming the John Wayne epic movie, *Donovan's Reef*. The scenery here reminded me partly of Florida, partly of Colorado, but there also was something unique in these islands, a tropical look of plastic plants and mountains that seemed to be painted backdrops for some old Dorothy

Lamour flick. We had lunch at the Sheraton Kauai, a buffet of baked pork and the usual salads found in every buffet line. The pineapple slices were fresh and tasty, but the pork was cured in a way that seemed strange to my Southwestern tastes.

That evening we found our hotel excellent and reasonably priced. On the outer islands the merchants were not so hell-bent on gouging as in Honolulu, and the food was far better than we had eaten previously. A swim in the ocean seemed an excellent way to end the day, but we found this an unpleasant experience when we went out. The temperature was chilly, and there was the smell of dead fish everywhere. Moreover, the beach tilted sharply into the ocean, and was covered with various types of debris that had washed ashore. People raised in a swimming-pool culture find the ocean, for all the mystique about it generated by poets and sailors, a disappointment. A swimming pool is cleaner, better smelling, and its bottom far more predictable.

We began the next day, Monday, as we did the previous day—by boarding an airplane, this time to fly to the island of Hawaii. On the way we paused at the island of Maui; we did not disembark, but at least could later say we had been on the four major islands that make up the state of Hawaii. Arriving at last at Kona, we were taken to town by bus. We drove along a road running through a lava bed which was bleak and harsh and out of which somehow grew plants with the most beautiful flowers imaginable. The island of Hawaii is volcanic in origin; it also is the newest of the islands and the biggest, and everywhere we looked we were reminded that the three large peaks on the island were capable of spewing out the porous lava.

We arrived at what our tour brochure called a "resort hotel" to find that at 10:30 in the morning our room had not as yet been cleaned from its last resort guests. Again we felt that terrible frustration known to those caught in the impersonal system, for there was nothing we could do but sit in the lobby and look at our suitcases. We had no car and no place to go until noon. We did content ourselves by making a token protest to the representative of the company responsible for our tour, but he did not get very excited; there was nothing he could do, and, after all, it was many miles to Honolulu and the home office. So we sat and waited. Children, however, enjoy many benefits not known to adults. They could—and did—change to their swimsuits in the lobby restrooms, then they went to the pool to swim, dive, and splash until our room was ready at last.

I spent the hour that followed musing about the architecture of hotels in Hawaii. Most of them have no doors or even walls on two sides of their lobbies. They are open to the street on one side and to the courtyard and pool on the other, for there is no need to heat them in the winter or to cool them in the summer. The lobby is left open so that the tradewinds can blow through. This simultaneously is "romantic" as well as inexpensive. And the islands are quite cool so long as you sit in the shade and do no exercise. The temperature generally is eighty degrees, but the humidity is about the same or higher; therefore, if you work in the sun you get very hot. At last I was interrupted in my musing by a bellboy who said our room was ready and that our suitcases had been taken there.

After lunch we were fetched by bus and taken to the dock in Kona. There we boarded the *Captain Cook,* a fair-sized cruising boat with glass panels in the bottom for observing the fish. This took us for what our brochures described as a "narrated excursion along the Kona Coast." Actually this side of the island of Hawaii, the leeward side, gets little rain and is surprisingly barren. And there was no beach of white sand, just lava flows right down to the ocean. As we cruised southward, however, we noted very expensive "resort hotels" where the only swimming possible was in pools.

After an hour we arrived at Kealakekua Bay (I never learned to pronounce these names). There we saw the monument erected at the spot where Captain James Cook landed in 1778; this English sailor was the discoverer of the islands, which then boasted a native monarchy. The following year Cook returned to Hawaii and there was killed. A small white marble shaft marks the site of discovery. Nearby in the bay our boat anchored, and swimming was allowed from the back of the boat. However, the crew warned us against trying to reach shore, for the bottom of the area just down from the beach was covered with what they called pin cushions, an aquatic plant much like a cactus. This spiny marine life caused infections in anyone who brushed against it, and the coral would cut deeply. Nancy and Richard had brought their swimsuits, and they jumped happily into this sheltered area to splash and swim. The crew of the *Captain Cook* provided face masks and snorkels, and they threw bread into the water to attract the fish. Richard commented that he found the experience "the best swim of my life," and Nancy allowed that it was "very good."

That evening we walked from our hotel the five blocks into Kona to do some shopping and sightseeing, but we found little that we wanted to buy. Of special interest to us were the wooden fish for sale in some of the small stores; these were imported from various Pacific islands, especially Tonga, and were exquisitely fashioned. However, the prices more than matched the beauty, and we decided that foot-long fish were not worth thirty to fifty dollars.

Tuesday morning we checked out of our hotel following breakfast and waited for the tour bus that was to take us around the island of Hawaii. The food in Kona we found to be more like that in Honolulu than that on the island of Kauai—high priced and not of good quality. The bus made stops at several hotels before it finally was loaded, and then we set out. First we climbed up the side of the island to about one thousand feet above sea level; at this height the foliage thickens considerably, for the rainfall here is much greater than near the ocean. Here at this level we found the coffee trees for which Kona is famous.

Our bus driver, a Japanese-American, stopped when we reached this level to explain to us about Kukua nuts. These are used to make necklaces, bracelets, and other types of jewelry for sale to tourists. When these are taken from the tree, the grower punches a tiny hole through the stem into the interior of the nut, then buries them to allow the ants to eat out the insides. Then the nuts are unearthed to be polished, sanded, and made into jewelry. By the time they reach the market, these Kukua nuts are a deep rich black and look like lacquerware.

On the bus with us we met some New Zealanders and fell into conversation with them. They urged us most strongly to visit their homeland, which they assured us was very beautiful. There also were two Mexican couples on this tour. They apparently were following the same itinerary as we, and were staying at the most expensive hotel in each of the cities we visited. We also met an Australian couple on this bus. Laura and I tried to talk with them about their country, but we had little success for they were more interested in questioning us about the United States. They said they had been touring our country for several weeks and were strongly thinking about immigrating, for they were looking for a place where the taxes were not as high as in Australia and where it would be pleasant to live. These comments disheartened us somewhat, for it implied that Australia might not be a good alternative for discontented Americans. We decided at last, however, that this couple might just be disgruntled and did not really typify Australia. We were not going to give up our trip on the basis of what one couple said.

As we drove around the southern tip of the island of Hawaii—the most southerly point in the United States—we were astonished to find housing developments going up right in the middle of lava-flow routes from the eruptions of just a few years ago. This was where lava had flowed like a river from the nearby volcano—and where future eruptions were obviously going to flow. This was as different—even weird—an area as ever I have seen anywhere on earth; it was broken and cracked, undulating like a wild river frozen in tumultuous passage, and all black for no trees or vegetation of any kind grew there as yet. However, the streets laid out on these lava flows have beautiful names: Orchid Lane, Ocean View Boulevard, and so forth. Apparently if anyone is going to sell junk real estate, the first necessity is to give the streets fancy names.

After pausing at one of the black sand beaches, which the tourist brochures pictured so lavishly and which we found to be nothing more than pulverized lava not really fit for beach lounging, we arrived at last at Volcano National Park. This natural wonder is in the immediate vicinity of a live volcano, one which erupted violently just a year ago, and here we were served a good lunch in a dining room that overlooked a massive crater; in this we could see steam venting up through cracks in the surface as underground water came into contact with hot areas. After the meal we were driven through the park. Almost everywhere steam was venting, and the cold lava flows looked so new as to remind us that eruptions had occurred just a short while before. Yet we were repeatedly warned by our guide that federal park regulations forbade one's picking up anything as a souvenir; not even one tiny bit of lava could be carried off. This rule obviously is necessary at federal parks, but here there is enough lava for every American—man, woman, and child—to have several chunks and there would still be enough left to serve as a park.

Toward late afternoon we arrived at the city of Hilo, and there we visited an orchid nursery and were taken to view Rainbow Falls. Both were interesting although in different ways, as was a tourist store we stopped at to view workers weaving baskets, purses, hats, and knickknacks from the broad leaves of one of the tropical plants. Naturally we were offered an opportunity to purchase the output "at factory prices"—which were as high as, if not higher than, the prices in Honolulu.

We were the last to leave this bus that evening, for everyone else aboard was spending the night in Hilo and we were going to the airport for a late evening flight to Honolulu. On the way to the airport we talked to the driver about the large number of Japanese tourists we had seen in Hawaii. He told us that the Hawaiian merchants like the Japanese tourists, for these Orientals normally spend more money for souvenirs than do Americans. The Japanese tourist, said the bus driver, wants to take home presents to every member of his family, and he will spend freely to do so. In fact, the driver told us, the average Japanese tourist tips more than does the average American tourist.

That evening we returned to Honolulu—but not to our two hotel rooms. The hotel at which we were staying did not have two rooms available and therefore gave us a penthouse suite. This was one huge room with a balcony that overlooked the ocean. We could only conclude that it is all right in Honolulu to have four people in a room if that room is a penthouse suite; otherwise it somehow violates city law.

During the next two days we talked to several Hawaiians about the Japanese tourists and learned that not everyone in the islands is happy with the new reality. There are Americans who have worked for years at some hotel or restaurant and have risen to a position of assistant manager or a similar level; now suddenly they are being fired and replaced with someone who speaks Japanese and who better understands the Japanese psyche. We also were told that Japanese businessmen are buying real estate in Hawaii at a rapid clip; on this land they are building hotels to cater to the Japanese tourist boom. They also are buying or building golf courses in Hawaii (golf apparently is the latest craze in Japan; people there are paying astronomical sums for membership in certain country clubs, and the businessmen investing in Hawaii feel the visiting Japanese tourists will pay well to play while in the islands on vacation). What the Japanese could not capture at gunpoint in World War II they now apparently are purchasing. I guess this is a much preferable means of conquest.

On Wednesday morning, after an overpriced but undertasty breakfast, we took a tour of the city of Honolulu by bus.

This hauled us rapidly by the University of Hawaii, Manoa Valley, downtown Honolulu, Chinatown, the Civic Center, and Iolani Palace. If you blinked your eyes at any of these you missed them entirely—although the glossy brochure about this tour implied that you would see them at leisure. At one spot on this tour, a mission of some denomination or another, there was the grass shack where Robert Louis Stevenson had once stayed—along with a souvenir shop and a snack shop, both of which boasted prices that would have bankrupted Stevenson in short order. At this place we had thirty minutes and more to wait and browse and eat. The other place at which we had plenty of time to look was Punchbowl National Cemetery. The many rows of crosses, each marking the grave of some American who died for his country, reminded us that freedom is never free.

That afternoon, gluttons for punishment that we were, we went on a cruise of Pearl Harbor. According to our itinerary, provided by our tour agent, only one vessel made this cruise, but so many tourists had purchased tickets that three boats were pressed into service. The captains of these three then got into a race to see who could make the roundtrip in the shortest possible time; inasmuch as the waves were cresting at six to eight feet, this made for a rough cruise during the time we were on the open sea.

During the part of the cruise actually inside Pearl Harbor, there was a recorded commentary about the events of December 7, 1941. The announcer evinced a slick—but not very convincing—patriotism and maudlin sympathy for those who had died during that sneak attack. Whenever someone wraps himself in the flag, he generally is a scoundrel, and the directors of this tour, the ones responsible for this commentary, certainly would so qualify. About one-third of the tourists on this cruise were Japanese. I noticed that they were extremely busy clicking their cameras as we passed the memorial to the sunken *Arizona* and the other spots bombed thirty-three years ago.

That evening, our last in Hawaii, we resisted the call of

our tour guide to partake of a genuine luau—for just fourteen dollars apiece. I was amazed that Americans visiting Hawaii (or Mexico for that matter) will spend exorbitant sums to sample what supposedly is the life of the local resident. The bus to go to the luau that evening was full of people who had paid fourteen dollars each for what supposedly is a native party. But the average Hawaiian who goes to a genuine luau spends little but time (as does the average Mexican going to a fiesta). The Hawaiian of the past, the one the average tourist is trying to imitate, lived in a grass shack because that was free, costing only a little of his time to make. He would harvest pineapple at the same cost, run down a wild hog, catch a few fish, and the women would cook—all free. Today the American tourist will spend a ridiculous sum to live in a grass shack—if it is air-conditioned and as comfortable as a regular hotel in New York City. The grass shack of today has sides made of cement blocks and a roof of plastic, but it "looks" native, and that is what counts. The luau for which the tourist pays is about as authentic as the grass shack, and probably about as digestible.

On Thursday morning we packed our suitcases and departed for the airport. As we waited to board the plane, we talked about our impressions of Hawaii. I personally was very disappointed with Hawaii. *Plastic* is the word that comes to my mind. Perhaps I see the fiftieth state this way because I had expected something different, something more romantic. What I found was a synthetic tourist trap engaged in packaging and merchandising something that does not exist: a South Seas paradise. The prices were much too high, the food was generally of poor quality, the hotels gouging, the service shoddy. True, the frangipani plants do have flowers, the rains come and rainbows follow, and the tropical splendor is there; but everywhere I got the feeling that the tour guides were moving people in to see each new "attraction" as rapidly as possible so that they could be moved out quickly and more tourists brought rapidly in so they could be moved out and more tourists. . .

Laura disagreed. She found the scenery beautiful and the sights unforgettable. She enjoyed browsing in the shops, even those filled with tourist merchandise, for it was sufficiently different to be a pleasure. Nor did she resent the way our tour director had scheduled us in and out of attractions, for we could not have seen so much of Hawaii in just five days otherwise. Richard and Nancy agreed with their mother. They enjoyed swimming in the ocean. They had learned to body surf and longed to get surfboards and try "hanging ten" with the college kids who crowded the beaches. Richard had purchased a ukulele and a Hawaiian shirt, while Nancy had a muu-muu and a charm bracelet.

On one point Laura and I did agree strongly. For someone visiting Hawaii, a tour such as we were on is an excellent introduction to the islands. Moreover, by purchasing a package tour you escape the anger of paying for each of the items on the tour piecemeal; you do not realize just what it costs you to take the Captain Cook Cruise or how expensive it is to watch your captain race some other captain in and out of Pearl Harbor. Rather, you choke just once when you pay some travel agent back on the mainland. But that is before you leave, and it does not interfere with your vacation in Hawaii.

At the airport on that Thursday morning we reported to the Canadian Pacific Airlines terminal to board our plane to Fiji. We were supposed to board this flight just after noon, but somehow it was delayed coming in from Vancouver and we did not get off until about 3:00 P.M. The plane was a DC-8 and the food excellent. The flight lasted seven hours, and we gained an additional two hours, thanks to our travel westward. Also, we crossed the international date line, and thus when we landed that evening at 8:00, it was Friday.

Arriving at Nadi (pronounced Nandi) Airport, we were directed to officials who checked our passport and then asked for our smallpox-vaccination record. With sinking heart we told them that we had been assured we did not need any kind of vaccination. However, the health officer, a Fiji woman in the uniform of a nurse, told us we had to be inoculated for smallpox or else we could not enter the country. To refuse meant we would have to remain in the lounge of the Nadi Airport until we could arrange a flight to Sydney. We therefore agreed to be vaccinated.

The nurse and a guard took us from the customs area across the airport, which was being expanded and thus was under construction, to what passed for the health office. There I paid a dollar each for the four of us to have the inoculation. While the nurse was administering these, I was talking with another American, also awaiting vaccination, and failed to notice that the nurse violated good medical practice. She did not wipe our arms with alcohol, and, far worse, she used the same needle on the four of us, along with our fellow American and a Canadian lad. Looking back on this incident, which was to cause us much anguish, I suspect that the nurse and the guard simply pocketed the six dollars they charged for these shots.

By the time we returned to the customs area, collected our luggage, and had our passport stamped, it was past 9:00 P.M. We were very tired. In Oklahoma, where real time prevailed, it was almost 5:00 A.M., and we longed for bed. We hurried to catch the complimentary bus that took us to the Dominion International Hotel, where we had reservations. This "international standard" hotel charged us $26 for one room that in the United States would not cost much more than half this amount. And we learned that this $26 was in Fijian currency—and one dollar American exchanged for seventy-three cents in local money. Our beds that night cost us almost $36 American, but by the time we got to the hotel we would have paid even more for the pleasure of some place to sleep.

It was Saturday when we awakened, one week since we left home. No, not really a week, for we had lost a day crossing the international date line. Yet it was not thoughts about losing Thursday that roused me from sleep; rather, it was a sound I had not heard in many, many years—a rooster crowing. That and some other kind of bird making a sound straight out of a Tarzan movie. As the four of us went about the business of digging through suitcases for clothes for the day, Nancy looked in a closet and found supplies for making coffee and tea, along with a ceramic pot containing a heating coil inside it. Laura and I wanted coffee so she filled it with water, and I plugged it in. Nothing happened. I turned the plug around, but still it did not work. At last I phoned the desk clerk to say that the electricity was not on in that plug. He said he would send someone up to look at it. A few moments later a knock at our door announced the arrival of a bellboy, who took one look and informed us, in tones usually reserved for the mentally retarded, that we had not turned on the plug. We looked and found him correct. We had not turned it on; beside the plug was a switch for turning the current on or off for that plug. We thanked the bellboy, trying to hide our embarrassment, and eased him out the door. We found that in every room here and in Australia all electric plugs also had switches so the current could be turned on and off. Eventually we made ourselves a cup of coffee that morning, but then found we could hardly drink it. The brand of the instant coffee was familiar enough, but the taste definitely was not; the coffee was so wretched that we abandoned the effort and went downstairs to find breakfast.

Our hotel (or motel—the literature called it both) was very new, having opened only months previous to our arrival. We opened our front door and were on a veranda that ran to one end where stairs took us to ground level. Looking out, we saw mountains in the distance, cane fields nearby, palm trees swaying in the wind, and tropical vegetation growing all around. Workmen already were busy erecting another wing on the hotel.

Downstairs we found that some effort had been made to give the hotel a Fijian atmosphere. The office had a grass roof to make it look like a native *bure* ("hut"), while the restaurant-bar had no walls (much like the lobby of the hotels in Hawaii). The dining room was filled with Australians on holiday, as they call vacation. For breakfast Nancy ordered cereal, while the rest of us had hotcakes. However, Nancy found her milk somewhat sour, and we discovered that the syrup tasted as if it had been made from coconuts.

Next came the question of what to do for the day. Earlier we had read that roads of decent quality ran from Nadi to Suva, the major city on the eastern side of the island, and that this was the way to see Fiji. One brochure assured us that going by road would reveal to us typical village life, lovely jungle scenery, and unrivaled seascapes, that excellent scenes to be photographed would present themselves to us, and that we would be rewarded with opportunities to chat with Fijian people. We learned that there were three ways open to us to travel the road: by bus, by limousine, or by rental car. There were air-conditioned buses for tourists that stopped at all the resort areas, and there were buses used by the Fijians themselves, rattly old conveyances with every window open and crowded with a jumble of humanity along with a few chickens and even an occasional pig. We thought of all the possibilities and then called Avis to rent a car, a small Japanese two-door sedan with right-side drive. In this we set out.

Driving north, we found ourselves on a very narrow road pockmarked with holes. It curved around through fields of sugarcane bordered by tall pines and even an occasional banana tree. Periodically the road was crossed by railroad tracks, which generally ran parallel to it; these tracks are used by the narrow-gauge trains that haul the cane to the sugar mills. Every three or four miles we would come to a cluster of native houses that for the most part were European in design, but occasionally we saw a genuine *bure*. In these villages we saw women in printed blouses and long skirts. The men wore something that resembled the Scottish kilt but that was actually just a strip of cloth wound around them, we were told.

After driving for half an hour, we came to the town of Lautoka. Driving through it, we saw the waterfront with fishing boats and a few larger boats; on these the tourist could cruise to the Mamanuca and Yasawa islands, or he could arrange one-day trips to the very small islands nearby for snorkeling, sunning, and picnicking. In Lautoka we spotted a Fijian policeman wearing a white skirt and gracefully directing traffic with fluid motions that would make a ballerina envious. And here we noticed something else, the extremely large number of Indians. In fact, we learned that there were more people here who had come from India (or descended from those who had) than there were native Fijians. The Fijians we saw were a very tall, well-formed race; they still smiled easily and spoke English with a pleasant sing-song British accent. The Indians were surly and grasping, a look of hatred being the predominant expression we noted. At one place in town we saw a white mosque that had small towers with bulbous tops at each corner. After parking the car, we shopped for souvenirs. Richard found a small outrigger canoe for eighty-five cents; the same sold in Nadi for $2.50—and in Hawaii for $4.50. Perhaps Lautoka was sufficiently off the tourist track that its prices were yet reasonable.

Next we retraced our path to our motel and then south into Nadi itself. This was on the beaten path, and within a remarkably short time we convinced ourselves that we had seen all we wanted of it. Nadi is a duty-free shopping area, but there really was nothing we wanted there. We parked to discuss the question of what to do next when, to our astonishment, every storekeeper and merchant began locking his shop. We learned from a passerby that in Fiji all business comes to a halt Saturday at noon and nothing opens again until Monday morning. Yet we had not flown all this distance to sit in a motel room with no television and swim in a freshwater pool for a day and a half. Why not, we asked ourselves, use the weekend for travel and get on to Australia? A phone call to Qantas Airlines brought news that we could move our reservation forward from tomorrow to today and that we could leave at 5:00 that afternoon for Sydney. While we ate lunch at the Nadi TraveLodge (which we learned is an Australian-owned corporation), we reflected on our experiences in Fiji.

We concluded that some of the workers at the airport had gouged us by forcing us to take a shot and had pocketed the money. Also, we noted that all the tourist literature about Fiji had said there is no tipping in these islands, but that every Fijian with whom we had any dealings had his hand out for a tip. And in the normal tourist places the prices of curios and souvenirs were outrageous. Another thought that intruded on me was that Fiji smelled foreign in the same way I recall Mexico City and Tokyo smelling foreign. It just was not the same as the smells in an American city. We concluded that Fiji within five years will be as plastic as most other tourist traps in the world. It will be filled with hotels boasting *bures,* but the sides will be made of reinforced concrete and the roofs of plastic grass, and the souvenirs will be imported from Hong Kong.

We checked out of the Dominion Hotel and drove to the airport to return our rent-a-car. From the clerk at the Avis desk I learned that the airport bank was open (as one would be at every major airport we visited; these do not keep regular banking hours, but are open almost all the time for the convenience of travelers). That morning at the hotel we had exchanged a traveler's check for Fijian money, but we had not spent all of this. Therefore we went to the bank, and I emptied my pockets to get Australian currency. However, both Richard and Nancy expressed a desire to keep one of each denomination of Fijian coin as a souvenir; this they did: a 50¢, 20¢, 10¢, 5¢, 2¢, and 1¢ coin.

As our Qantas flight rolled down the runway, we looked back with little regret at having to leave. Laura had not enjoyed it, for she prefers her food to be sanitary and the drinking water trustworthy. Moreover, all four of us were unhappy at having had to take a smallpox vaccination after having been told that this would not be necessary. Yet on this flight I learned that we actually had been quite lucky. Sitting next to me was a Japanese businessman who had been attending a conference in Nadi. As we chatted during the flight, comparing our thoughts about Fiji, I told him about our inoculation for smallpox. He then told me that he had taken a smallpox shot before leaving his home in Tokyo, but when he arrived at Nadi he was told he had to have a cholera shot. For this he had paid a Fijian dollar—and then had been ill during the three days of his conference in Nadi. I guess it was just as well that we had not had a smallpox vaccination. Otherwise we might have had to take a cholera shot so that the night nurse could have made her few dollars, and we would have spent the next three days sick rather than flying toward Sydney.

Looking back toward the island as we departed, I could see lights glowing everywhere in the dusk. And it was getting dark despite the earliness of the hour, for here in the Southern Hemisphere late in May the sun sets early; this part of the world was approaching its shortest day of the year. No, we felt no regret at leaving Fiji. And we were in a fever of excitement that at long last we were approaching Australia, a country we had wanted to see for so many years.

III.

Tasmania

I AM NOT certain just what we expected on our flight with Qantas. We had seen the commercials for this airline on television for years, the one where the koala bear climbs aboard a 747 while a sad voice, supposedly his, tells us that he hates Qantas for bringing so many tourists to Australia. Probably because of this both Richard and Nancy wanted more than anything else on their vacation in Australia to see and hold a koala. And probably because of this they both had asked our travel agent to schedule us aboard Qantas at some point on our flight.

In reading the literature about Australia we had learned that Qantas is the second oldest airline in the world, starting in 1920 in the town of Winton, which is in the central-western part of the state of Queensland. This was the Queensland and Northern Territory Aerial Services; the initials spell QANTAS (whose official name now is Qantas Empire Airways).

We did not board a 747, however. Rather it was a Boeing

707, but the five-hour flight did prove to be a real adventure. Again we gained two hours, making us nine hours earlier (but one day later) than God's time at home. We departed at 5:00 P.M., and as this was a dinner flight we expected to be eating within at least an hour. We quickly learned that the Australians, who were far in the majority aboard, had other ideas. They were still on holiday, at least until they got to Sydney, and they intended to make the most of their last few hours. They began ordering drinks and yet more drinks and then still more drinks. The stewardesses apparently were accustomed to this, for they made no real attempt to serve any food until most of the passengers were in an alcoholic fog. After two hours passed and no food had appeared, Laura finally managed to stop one of the stewardesses coming down the aisle with a tray loaded with empty bottles and ask for something for the children. "Would Coke and biscuit be all right?" the girl asked. Laura nodded. At this point she felt anything would be all right although neither she nor I knew what the biscuit would prove to be. When the tray came, we discovered that a biscuit is a cookie (and the Coke was bottled in Perth).

Qantas did not have a section of the plane reserved for nonsmokers, and again I could inhale more tobacco than when I had puffed my pipe. It had been seven days since I had smoked, and the smell of tobacco was tantalizing, but I gritted my teeth and resisted the temptation to ask the stewardess to bring me a pack of anything to smoke. Looking around, I noticed that the Australians returning from Fiji, with its duty-free shopping, were almost all bringing back two cartons of cigarettes along with a gallon of whiskey. In this they were little different from the Americans we had seen crossing the Mexican border when we lived in Arizona; all wanted to save as much as possible on the impossibly high taxes all governments seem to impose on tobacco and alcoholic beverages. In years past my wife and I both had resented these taxes, but now, as neither of us smoked and rarely drank anything other than a little wine occasionally, we were not too unhappy about this.

Our stomachs kept rumbling, but still no food was produced. We were diverted for a time by the stewardesses passing out customs declaration forms. We had been asked to do the same thing coming to Fiji. The Australian form, as well as the one for Fiji, had us give our name, address, occupation, point of departure, length of stay projected in the country, our passport number, and our flight number. Both Richard and Nancy insisted on filling out their own and felt very important affixing their signatures to an official document.

I have always been suspicious of restaurants where the patrons are encouraged to drink a great amount before any food is produced, and thus I grew worried at what would be produced from the galley if trays ever were brought. Also, I began to wonder if this was typical of Australians: that they would rather drink than eat. My fears were put to rest at last, and the meal proved a delightful exception, one worthy of the wait: a salad of Lobster Paradise, and entrée of Mignonettes of Beef Forestiére, croquette potatoes, buttered peas, cream caramel, cheese, and coffee. Looking about me, I was struck quite forcefully by the pervasive American influence so many miles from home. Sitting beside me was a businessman from Japan who was smoking Marlboro cigarettes; we were flying on an Australian airline but in a Boeing 707; Richard and Nancy were drinking Coca-Cola bottled in Perth; and on our trays were Kraft butter and Kraft cheese.

During the last part of our flight, which was in the middle of this delicious dinner, the weather turned so rough that Laura's coffee spilled in her cream caramel, while on the other side of me the Japanese businessman spilled his wine in his lap. This proved to be a rainstorm of high intensity, and as we landed at Sydney the winds were in the vicinity of sixty miles an hour. This was late in May, or autumn, in Australia, but our welcome reminded us of the spring storms in Oklahoma that often spawn high winds and even tornadoes. Later we learned that this particular storm had dumped many inches of snow in the mountains of southeastern Australia and had brought the worst floods in many years to many parts of New South Wales and Queensland.

As we disembarked in Sydney, thankful to be on solid, stable ground once again, Laura and I reflected that neither Canadian Pacific Airlines nor Qantas had taken care of us as Braniff did on our flight to Hawaii—and in our opinion Braniff has the poorest service of almost any airline in the United States.

Retrieving our luggage at the new international airport at Sydney, we really could not tell by looking that we were in a foreign country. And customs proved extremely easy to pass through; we had our passport stamped, stated that we had nothing illegal to declare, and were waved through. With our luggage loaded on a push cart similar to those in grocery stores at home, we proceeded to the bank; this was open despite the lateness of the hour (it was about 9:00 P.M. by this time). For a $100.00 money order, we received $66.61 —minus six cents for a stamp that had to be affixed to the paper. This stamp tax is exactly the same as the stamp tax against which American colonists rebelled two hundred years ago. This transaction, which netted us $66.55 Australian for $100.00 American, brought home forcefully to us how the dollar had slid because of the two devaluations. In reading about Australia, we had found that three years ago the two currencies were approximately equal. Two years ago, following the first devaluation, the rate of conversion was $1.19 American to $1.00 Australian; this then dropped to $1.42 American to $1.00 Australian just a year ago. And now, with the dollar floating in value, the rate of exchange was $1.5011 American to $1.00 Australian.

Shaking our heads in sadness, we turned our thoughts to finding a place to sleep for the night. Inasmuch as we were a day ahead of our original schedule, we had no reservation for the night. There at the airport, however, was a desk to handle just such problems; a girl informed us that she could make a reservation for the night, which she did at the Randwick Motel. We did not question the cost, for we were tired and the hour was late; instead we took the slip of paper from her and asked about taxis. "Oh, don't pay for a taxi," she told us. "Taxis are too dear. You can get on the air porter service at the main entrance."

At the main entrance we found it raining hard outside, but a friendly porter helped us aboard the bus. During the ride into town, which was extremely crowded, I looked at the town and saw Pittsburgh, New York City, Los Angeles—every big city; they are all remarkably similar.

That night we were too tired to note much of anything about our motel except that it was cold. However, the next morning, Sunday, several things quickly became apparent. The Randwick House Motor Inn is part of the MFA, or Motel Federation of Australia, a chain of motels linked together by a telex reservation system, which, according to the inn's printed literature, should be about the equivalent of the Holiday Inns and Ramada Inns, with which most Americans are familiar. Such was not the case, however.

I had heard that Australians tend to be "knockers," as they call it, meaning they are critical of most things. And subsequently I found in my conversations that indeed they do tend to be a little cynical. Well, I do not mean to be a knocker, but the Randwick House, if typical of Australian motels, was not an auspicious beginning. Just a few days later in Tasmania I would look back with longing for the quality of the Randwick. Yet this establishment was cold. It was seedy. The bathroom looked like something from a quarter of a century before. As Laura pointed out, the hot- and cold-water faucets in the bathroom sink were separate, and thus water could not be mixed together as we are accustomed to doing in America. And there was no built-in closet, just a clothes chest (wardrobe) standing in one corner. Moreover, the sheets had been starched and ironed, something that is far worse in actuality than it sounds when reading about it.

Finally we discovered one other sad fact. Before we left home someone who had been to Australia warned us that the toilet paper was extremely rough, not cottony soft as Americans have come to expect. This also proved true.

This morning we also learned that the portfolio on the dresser in Australian motels is not there just to hold stationery and a directory of motel services, even a flyswatter, as is the case in the United States. Here the portfolio also contains an additional item, a breakfast menu. This the guest is supposed to fill out by 8:00 the previous evening and turn in to "reception," as they call the clerk at the front desk. The next morning the breakfast that the guest orders is delivered to his room on a tray. This practice of filling out a breakfast menu and having the food brought to the room is a carryover from the not so distant past when a continental breakfast was served complimentary to all guests at Australian motels and hotels. Now the charge generally is about one dollar for this service.

The continental-breakfast menu was divided into four sections: juice, with a choice of tomato, orange, or pineapple; fruit, with a selection of pineapple (much of which is grown in Queensland), fresh fruit in season, and stewed fruit; cereal, and the choice here was "Rice Bubbles," Corn Flakes, or All Bran; and beverage, which meant tea, coffee, cold milk, or hot milk. When you check tea or coffee, you have to indicate whether you want it black or white; white means you want milk in it.

Inasmuch as we were ignorant of the local custom of ordering breakfast the evening before, we had not filled out these forms and no food was brought to us. We did venture forth in search of the motel restaurant, as we would at home, and then were told what we should have done. Our host apparently saw the shock on our face and took pity on us, telling us to take a table and fill out one of these order forms apiece. We ordered the continental breakfast and soon were munching away on Corn Flakes. These were made by Kellogg, and they taste the same all over the world—which is to say, there is about as much flavor in the cardboard box containing the flakes as in the flakes themselves.

On this same menu, however, there was the statement, "For those with a heartier appetite, may we suggest the addition of one of these items to your continental breakfast." There followed such readily identifiable things as eggs and bacon, eggs and sausage, and "minit steak" and eggs. Below this, however, was a list of things that came as a real cultural shock: spaghetti on toast, baked beans on toast, creamed corn on toast, and "mushrooms sautes." We ordered the sausage and eggs for an additional sixty cents, but the pork sausage, when it arrived, was not even distantly related to any pork sausage we had ever eaten anywhere in the United States; it was closer to some kind of frankfurter. And with our eggs came fried tomatoes, another item not normally served for breakfast in Oklahoma. However, I tried both the sausage and the tomatoes and found them to be better than they sounded. This breakfast of juice, fruit, cereal, coffee, eggs, sausage, toast—and tomatoes—cost $1.60 Australian (or $2.40 American) and started us into our Australian venture thinking about the fact that we indeed were in a different country. Richard and Nancy, both of whom dislike tomatoes intensely, were ready to believe that a country where people ate fried tomatoes for breakfast must be degenerate. As for me, I pondered spaghetti on toast as a way to start the day. What next?

Next came checkout time. I discovered that the night's lodging came to twenty dollars, and my simple formula of two dollars Australian equals three dollars American told me that our room had cost us thirty dollars; a room in a Holiday Inn would not have cost nearly so much and would have been of higher quality. And this was not a wretched inn in a poor part of town; in fact, it was directly across the street from the Randwick racetrack and served a good clientele.

In talking with the innkeeper, I inquired about the best means of getting to the airport. He suggested a taxi, so we telephoned for one—and learned that an additional twenty-five cents is added when you call for a taxi rather than hail one that is cruising. The ride to the airport to catch our flight to Launceston, Tasmania, took us through part of Sydney, but we soon were on a freeway that looked just like freeways at home. The gasolines I saw advertised were Mobil, Esso, Shell, Caltex, and BP (British Petroleum), while many of the other signs advertised products familiar to most Americans. The city itself, now that I saw it in daylight with no rain falling, looked just like any large American city.

In boarding this taxi, Laura and the children got into the back seat, while I sat in the front with the driver (and in Australia I do not recall ever seeing a male passenger sitting by himself in the rear seat; always the man sits in the front seat with the driver—just as he is expected to help manhandle the luggage). When I saw that the fare would be about $3.75 or so, I asked why I had been told to take the airport bus the evening before.

"Probably because the clerk at the air terminal did not realize you had your family with you," I was told. My fare on the airport bus had been $1.25, Laura's was $1.25, and the children had ridden for seventy-five cents each, a total of four dollars. Also, I asked about the price of hotels and motels and was told that downtown hotels cost no more than the Randwick House. According to our driver, we had been directed to the Randwick because it would pay a referral fee to the people at the airport who had made our reservation.

When we arrived at the airport, we were not taken to the new international terminal, for this time our flight was domestic. Arriving at this building, we found that Ansett Airlines and Trans-Australian Airlines, the two major domestic carriers, each had a separate building. Inasmuch as we were flying first to Melbourne on TAA, we arrived at that building—and were astonished to find a terminal similar to a Greyhound bus terminal of fifteen to twenty years ago. It was a real shock to us, particularly to Richard and Nancy who had grown to expect airport terminals that looked nice.

In fairness, I do point out that a new domestic terminal is under construction in Sydney at this time.

As we boarded the plane for Melbourne, which was a 727, we were surprised that there was no searching of passengers or of their carry-on luggage (just as there had not been at Nadi, Fiji). However, there was a great amount of pushing and shoving, far more so than at any other airport I had been in; the plane was filled to capacity, but all seats were assigned so I saw no real reason for the hurry. In looking about at my fellow passengers, I noticed that they looked very much like the same class that would ride the bus at home. And I could not help but notice—I was compelled to notice—several people whose breath would fell a wombat at thirty paces. On this plane there were four rows of seats for passengers who did not smoke, but immediately after we were airborne the other passengers began puffing so furiously that a nicotine haze filled the entire compartment. All I had to do was inhale in order to become dizzy. And the stewardesses immediately began racing back and forth serving alcoholic beverages. The equivalent of our bars do not open in Australia on Sunday, and these people were getting something down while they had the opportunity.

At last a stewardess came to ask what we wanted to drink, and we ordered coffee—much to our regret. For years I have heard people from England say that in the United States we do not know the proper way to make tea. Well, the Australians reciprocate by not knowing how to make coffee. They use instant, and they make the brew strong. The dominant brand apparently is Nescafe, but I here venture a personal opinion that the coffee is really charcoaled, ground kangaroo dung, not anything that is grown on a coffee tree. Normally both Laura and I drink our coffee black, but unable to get that down we filled it with cream—and still were unable to drink it.

The stewardess offered Richard and Nancy their choice of coffee, tea, or squash. I asked her what "squash" was, but her reply came in such a thick British accent that I could not understand her. Richard took some and told me it was either lemonade or limeade, he was not certain which. Nancy preferred to be on the safe side and asked for a Coke; to my surprise the stewardess charged fifteen cents for it.

Richard was sitting by a window and I was beside him. In the row ahead of us Nancy sat by a window with Laura on her right. Next to Laura was a very charming lady returning to her home in Melbourne. She and Laura fell into an easy conversation, for the lady wished to talk about her daughter who worked for Trans-Australian Airlines. This lady asked why our children were not in school, and when she learned we were American she explained the Australian school system. In Australia the children begin the school year in January. There are three vacations during the year: two weeks in April, two weeks in September, and five weeks at Christmas. Naturally she asked Laura where we would be spending our "holiday" in Australia. Learning that we intended to see most of the continent, she expressed regret that she had seen so little of her own country. But she was returning from a holiday in New Zealand. We concluded that Australians are no better at seeing their own country first than are Americans.

On this flight from Sydney to Melbourne the clouds were very thick when we took off, preventing our forming any impression of the land. Suddenly, however, there was a break in the cover, and below we could see the Snowy Mountains, which indeed were covered with snow. The recent rainstorms, which had flooded much of New South Wales and Queensland, had dumped precipitation in these mountains in the form of snow. Seeing this, the lady beside Laura commented that Australia was experiencing "the most unusual weather in years." I believe that everywhere we have ever visited the weather has been "unusual." In fact, I have come to believe that the weather never is normal anywhere at any given time.

Tullamarine Airport in Melbourne is very new and modernistic, having about as much regional or national flavor as most airports in the United States. The same architect apparently designs every one of them. We had lunch during our stopover and received yet another lesson in what our trip was going to cost us; life in Australia is not cheap, especially when you take into account the exchange rate. During this meal we noticed that the milk had a strange flavor. Then it dawned on us: the funny taste was the high butterfat content. The milk in Australia is rich in cream, and we no longer are accustomed to it. Later I would learn that much of the milk in Australia is not homogenized, and when it sits for a while the cream rises to the top. Older Americans who remember unhomogenized milk—and I am one of these—are astonished to find that this does not taste as good as we remember it.

The place where we grabbed this snack was not a fancy dining room but what in America we would call a coffeeshop or even a cafeteria, for it did have a serving line through which we pushed a tray. In Australia such a place is called a milk bar. And there we discovered another peculiarity of the country: water is not served at any meal unless you ask for it. I suppose this is due to the fact that local water supplies in Australia, along with those in most of the rest of the world, have not been safe to drink until recently. Any time you ask for water with a meal in an Australian restaurant, the waitress will comment, "Oh, you're a Yank." Apparently Americans are the only people who want to drink water with their meals. During the rest of our stay in Australia, we noticed that public water fountains were almost nonexistent.

At last our plane was called for our flight aboard Ansett Airlines to Launceston. At the boarding gate we were surprised to find search procedures in effect, including even an X-ray machine to look for concealed weapons. I talked with a guard at this gate about such searches, for I had assumed none was made in Australia. He told me that searches were now conducted on about thirty percent of the domestic flights and would extend to all as soon as the necessary equipment could be obtained. He also informed me that just the day before a passenger boarding a plane here in Melbourne had been discovered carrying a .25-caliber pistol.

"He was an immigrant chap," the guard asserted, an explanation which clearly implied that no real Australian would do such a thing. Little does he know. The crazies are everywhere apparently.

The flight from Melbourne south to Launceston did not take long. Melbourne is on the southeast side of the Australian continent, and Launceston is on the north side of the island of Tasmania; in between is Bass Strait. On our Boeing 727 this flight lasted less than an hour; there was just time for another cup of dreadful coffee and two "biscuits" wrapped in cellophane.

We sighted land about 4:35 that afternoon. Our descent toward Launceston's airport proved almost magical. We were flying just to the west of the Tamar River, which is very broad and stately at the coast and then narrows quickly to become little more than a creek some forty miles inland at Launceston. The land unfolding beneath us looked like something out of a child's storybook, an illustration for some tale about England. Everywhere there were fields of green grass broken by tall trees of the gum family; most of these were eucalyptus. Even the farmhouses had a stately Old World look about them. The scene grew even lovelier as we descended toward a landing south of town. All of us were extremely excited, anxious to begin seeing the real Australia at last.

At 4:45 we were at the terminal, but this far south late in May it already was dusk. And by the time we collected our baggage and checked out our automobile, it was too dark to see anything. Driving into town on the left side of the road in the English Ford we had rented proved difficult. The road was narrow, and it was pitch dark. I feared that if some emergency arose suddenly, I would react out of my lifetime habit of driving on the right side of the road, and do the exact opposite of what would help.

Without any incident, however, we arrived at the Trave-

Lodge Motel, where we had a reservation, the last one we had made before leaving home. Hereafter we would be on our own. After checking in, we went in search of the restaurant that we knew to be in the motel, and to our pleasant surprise it proved excellent. A T-bone steak dinner, including drink, cost only $2.65 (about $4.00 American), and the children were served theirs at half price. We later learned that almost all Australian restaurants serve children's portions of everything on their menus at half price, not just a children's portion of two or three selected items as is usually the case in the United States.

And to my surprise Richard and Nancy asked for hot tea with their meal. Apparently they had chosen to drink this beverage regularly. Laura and I talked about our problem, the wretched coffee we had been served everywhere, and concluded that we were going to be forced to drink tea. But I had hated hot tea since I was eight years old and had to drink some of it while I was in the hospital.

Back in our motel room we searched about and found the breakfast order forms. These we filled out in order to get something for our morning meal, and then I began reading the newspaper provided free with the room. From my reading of this Launceston newspaper I began to appreciate the fact that the problems facing Americans are not peculiar to us; they are worldwide. In Australia, from what I gleaned from the paper, the worries are inflation, high interest rates, the difficulties of purchasing a house, discontent among farmers, and the resentment of rural dwellers who believe they are being used to satisfy the needs of those in the cities. And Mr. Al Grassby, the minister of immigration running for re-election, wanted to drop the old barriers that kept colored people out of Australia.

On this note I put aside the newspaper, and we brewed a pot of tea in the electric pot provided—now that we understood how to turn on the switch. We needed this hot tea, for in the bathroom when we ran water for our bath we discovered that the window in this room was louvered and could not be closed. Late in May it is sufficiently cold in Tasmania that we needed what heat the tea provided.

The following morning, a Monday, we breakfasted in the room and checked out, determined to find a place where the bathroom at least was closed to the chill of the evening. First, however, we parked downtown so Laura could go to a beautyshop for a wash and set. While she was thus occupied, I took the children for a walk through town, stopping in Myers Department Store to look for a coat for Richard. We found nothing in this store, which is a chain operation extending throughout Australia. To my surprise, the prices were about the same as in an American store—and that was not allowing for the difference in exchange rates.

When Laura was through at the beautyshop, we checked into the Park Lane Motel. Laura decided to use the launderette facilities, and found the two ladies there as curious about her laundry as ladies are in America.

These things done, we went downtown. Launceston is composed of buildings constructed just before and just after the turn of the century, all very British, all well painted and clean, none over three or four stories high. Princess Square, with its fountain in the center and its autumn leaves, was particularly British and particularly lovely. Walking down the streets of this city, pausing to shop for a souvenir here and there, we paused at Dicky White's Bistro in the Launceston Hotel for lunch. We had the special of the day, which proved to be a kind of beef pie (stew served in a little round bowl with a crust on top of it); with this we had some of Tasmania's famous apple juice, which was cold and exceedingly good.

After lunch we set out to the north down the Tamar River valley. We took the east bank going up the Tamar Highway, as it is called, for this twenty-five-mile drive. The countryside proved beautiful beyond description. It was large hills rolling northward toward the sea with green pastures where sheep grazed peacefully, and on the land were ghost gums, a gum tree with white bark that peels and hangs in a most peculiar way. This was a sylvan scene of great tranquility. At last we came to the Batman Bridge, a modernistic structure that crosses the Tamar; the local citizens are extremely proud of this bridge, for it saves them an extremely long drive to get to the west side of the Tamar River. This land along the east and west sides of the Tamar reminded us of Southern California before housing developments replaced everything, but there was the difference of the weird trees, gum and eucalyptus. Even the air had a pungent tinge of gum in it.

Back in town we drove about, pausing at a game preserve (zoo) to look at the kangaroos and wallabies, laugh at the emus, and lament that there were no koalas there. Even the suburbs of Launceston were beautiful, most of the homes having red tile roofs. Nowhere did we see anything that looked like a slum section; even in the older sections of town the homes were meticulously cared for. The city reminded me of Calgary and Laura of Toronto; independently we both thought of Canada when seeking something for comparison. Each area has its subtle differences of culture, and this part of Australia is more similar to Canada than to the United States.

That evening as we prepared for bed, Laura asked if I could live here. Taking seriously a question like that really makes you think—and even to consider those subtle differences of culture I spoke about above. There are so many things that make up your own culture of which you no longer are closely aware—the brand of candy you like best, what kind of cigarettes to smoke, what type of shaving cream seems to go with your beard, to say nothing of preferences in gasoline, laundry soap, and dozens of other things.

The next day, while downtown, we noted the separate meat markets and green grocers; apparently the supermarket has not yet replaced all these things. How would we know which establishment to patronize except by trial and error—a slow process. And as I was looking at a list of motels in Tasmania, I noted that rates were quoted for room only, for B & B, and for B & B & Dinner. What, I wondered, was B & B? Apparently it was Bed and Breakfast, but I was not certain. Australians grow to maturity knowing about these things, absorbing them along with their baby food just as we Americans grow up knowing that Wheaties is the Breakfast of Champions and that Yogi Bear recommends Corn Flakes.

Could I live in Launceston? The answer seemed quite affirmative as we ate T-bone steak again that evening. This one cost about the equivalent of $4.50 American and seemed just a shade tough. Yet when I talked with an Australian there, I found he thought the beef very tender. At last the answer came clear to me: the beef here was grass-fed just before marketing and not as tender as grain-fed beef in America. For Australia the beef was excellent—as I later learned eating grass-fed beef elsewhere.

The following morning we set out to drive the Tasman Highway. This runs from Launceston to Hobart by way of the east coast of the island. As we studied the map for this section of the road, we assumed it would take us only about six hours to make the entire trip, but we did not realize how unique this highway would prove to be. The first section of the trip was from Launceston to Scottsdale and then to St. Helens, a distance of about 125 miles. This was over a road that wound and twisted through mountains. It strongly reminded me of West Virginia in some places, of Northern California-Southern Oregon in other places, and, where the clouds hung heavy in the mountains, of the Smoky Mountains of Tennessee and North Carolina. In some of the deep valleys in these mountains, we were surprised to find ferns growing lushly. And there was much logging of the giant gum trees, but reforestation was under way at these points. At several lookout points we were able to see the Pacific Ocean to the northeast, a magnificent scene.

St. Helens proved to be a resort town with miles of sheltered harbor, but this was late autumn for them and everything was boarded up. When we stopped for lunch, the proprietor of the establishment looked at us with distrust; apparently he took us for fools for touring at this time of year. But when he realized that we were Yanks—which was when we asked for water with our lunch—he warmed up considerably.

We next arrived at the town of St. Marys after driving just along a coastline of resort hotels and motels. The distance was only twenty-three miles, but the road was narrow and twisting. South of St. Marys, we drove through Elephant Pass (and some humorist had painted the *P* off the sign); we then arrived at a place where the countryside flattened out and we could make better time. This region reminded me in part of New England and a little of the island of Hawaii. From a distance the eucalyptus trees look like pines, and in several places we saw workers clearing the trees to open grazing land. Apparently this was a new project, for the gum trees look ten thousand years old. Cattle, both beef and dairy, were everywhere, along with sheep. And there were apple orchards here and there, but very little other agricultural endeavor that we could see. At every one of the villages along the way, we could see the fishing fleet, so apparently this is another source of income.

A major astonishment of this drive was to be ten or fifteen miles from the nearest village—and I do mean village, for there are no large cities along this route—and suddenly to find an eighteen-hole golf course. I stopped at one to find people playing; apparently they really like their golf. And the green fee at these public courses, I was told, was only fifty cents.

Passing through Swansea, another resort town which features sea and river fishing and where each November the state fishing championship is held, we arrived just at dark at a village named Orford. The motel at this place, part of one of the major chains, I leave mercifully nameless. It cost $20 Australian, which is the equivalent of $30 American, and was rotten. This entire area, I decided, is like Colorado in the summer and during skiing time; probably even the vacationing Australians get stuck. However, we could look out the window of our motel unit and see Maria Island offshore shrouded in mist. This was the site of a penal settlement in the first part of the nineteenth century, and I wondered how many

59

wretched men sat on that island looking at the spot where we now were housed; how many looked and longed to be standing where I was. Mt. Maria, rising 2,329 feet above the ocean, was obscured entirely.

In the Hobart newspaper that evening I read a complaint in the letter-to-the-editor section about how little was being spent on an art museum locally, while another story informed me that the final cost of the Sydney Opera House was $102,000,000 (Australian). The original cost of that project had been set at $9,000,000 Australian. Again I was finding things to be the same everywhere. The culture maniacs of this world always decry the unwillingness of the public to spend money and yet more money for this or that facet of culture—which will not support itself.

As to the weather, Laura and I were becoming more and more convinced that we had come at exactly the wrong time of year. Some three weeks from now it would be June 21, the longest day of the year at home but here the shortest. Moreover, my system was primed for the onset of summer. Like some plant, I had put out my summer leaves—along with my golf clubs and lawnmower—only to arrive here in late-autumn-turning-to-winter, and I was cold. All of us were cold!

And well we might be cold, for the Australians apparently do not know central heating as we do (nor do they have central air-conditioning, but that was not my problem just then). The TraveLodge Motel in Launceston had advertised itself as having central heat, as had the Park Lane in Launceston and our present motel in Orford, but at all three "central heat" consisted of a small electric-coil heater mounted on one wall. And the "thermostat" consists of an on-off switch; you turn it on until the room gets warm, and then you turn it off until the room gets too cool, and then you turn it on . . . However, at night there is no problem this time of year; you just turn the thing on and leave it, for it is cold; not only do you turn on the central heat, but also you snuggle under all the blankets available. This does allow you to stay warm—until you get out of bed. The bathrooms do not have central heat and are just plain cold. Apparently Australians are accustomed to less heat than Americans, for when I mentioned to some of them that I was cold they acted surprised.

According to the evening newspaper the national election had just seen the rascals in office get some comeuppance. The minister of immigration, Al Grassby, a self-styled intellectual and a liberal who wanted to lower the barriers of immigration in Australia to allow unlimited Asian entry, was voted out of office by his constituency and was making public outcries that his opponent was guilty of racism in the campaign. That probably is true, but then a majority of the voters apparently were racists—and in a democracy they should be represented by a racist. I suspect that if I lived in Australia and had no racial problem, I would vote against someone who wanted to import one. Especially would I vote that way after having seen what unlimited Asian immigration had done to Fiji; there immigrants from India outnumbered the native Fijians. Yet Mr. Grassby was making most unseemly noises about the injustice of democracy, insisting that he alone should tell the people of his district what their attitude toward immigration should be.

As we prepared for bed, Laura found that the lavatory in our bathroom had separate hot and cold spigots; therefore you could not turn on a little warm and a little cold, mix them properly, and hold your hands under warm water. Instead you turned on both and held your hands under first one, then the other, a most inconvenient arrangement. Just before we drifted off to sleep, Laura also noted that Australians apparently were having no difficulty understanding our brand of English, though we often found their speech unintelligible.

The next morning in Orford I heard roosters crowing somewhere nearby when I awakened at dawn, and I thought about the similarities and differences between Australia and the United States. Before we departed from home, several people had told us we would find it like the United States of twenty-five or thirty years ago. So indeed it was, but I was not convinced that this was good—or bad—as yet. The motels indeed were a quarter-century old, yet their prices were very contemporary on a dollar-for-dollar basis; however, with the rate of exchange so weighted against American currency, the price of lodging was ridiculously high. But food continued to be a bargain.

After settling our account with our host, we continued down the Tasman Highway until we arrived at the town of Sorell, which is seventeen miles from Hobart. Here we ventured onto the Arthur Highway, which would take us out on Forestier Peninsula. The mountains seemed now to loom quite large, although our map showed the biggest of these, Macgregor Peak, to be less than 2,000 feet high. All along this drive we caught magnificent glimpses of the nearby Tasman Sea.

And then we arrived at Eaglehawk Neck, a narrow spit of land that connects Forestier Peninsula with the Tasman Peninsula. When convicts first were brought to this island, they were housed at Port Arthur, whose ruins we were bound to see. Keeping them on the peninsula proved easy, for fierce dogs were allowed to roam loose at Eaglehawk Neck—which incidentally was the site of Abel Tasman's landing in 1642 on the island that would bear his name. The ruins at Port Arthur are a regular part of every tourist's itinerary on Tasmania, and pictures of them can be found readily. Today the peninsula is a tourist trap—and a fisherman's paradise. Here the prisoners too tough for Sydney's infamous jail were sent to repent of their sins, and repent they apparently did. This prison, which one visitor described as a "cage of unclean birds," was known widely as an "isthmus between earth and hell."

Retracing our route to Sorell, we continued our trip into Hobart. About five miles out of town we came to the city airport—and the freeway, the first we had encountered outside Sydney. On both sides of this easy drive we could see golf courses. As we continued toward town, however, we suddenly came upon the Tasman Bridge. This magnificent structure is more than a kilometer in length and ascends to a summit in the middle that easily allows ships of all sizes access to the Derwent River. Once on the Hobart (west) side of the Derwent, we were in the area known as the Queen's Domain, a vast park featuring a lovely botanical garden. In town we hunted out the motel we had selected from our guide to the establishments on the island. We completed the day by driving around town, viewing the famed Wrest Point Casino (where gambling is legal for anyone above age eighteen—with currency), the University of Tasmania, and even the botanical gardens.

That evening we tried to sort out our impressions, one of the most powerful and pervasive of which was the strong smell of the gum tree. On this day I had almost become ill from the smell. I could taste gum in the milk and smell it in the air. Even a drink of cold water was no pleasure, for in it, as in everything else, I could taste the gum tree. Whatever it is this tree puts out, it is STRONG.

Tasmania—"Tassie," as it is called locally—is more mountainous than I had thought. I had read that it had many mountains, but a look at topographical maps showed these to be only hills of four thousand feet or so. In short, I had thought Tasmania's mountains would be like those of the eastern part of the United States; to a Westerner, these seem only fair-sized hills. Immediately behind Hobart, Mt. Wellington rises 4,166 feet. That does not sound like a lot until you realize that all 4,166 feet rise above sea level; then Mt. Wellington becomes spectacular, which it is. Too, the mountains of Tasmania are crowded together and quite jagged, making them seem much like the Rockies in Colorado.

During our shopping this day I looked at the prices of appliances at Myers Department Store in Hobart and found them to be extremely high by American standards. A seventeen-inch television set—and this is black and white, for there is no color television in Australia as yet—sold for $240 Australian (or

$360 American), while a Whirlpool automatic washer cost $A295. Food prices do seem far more reasonable, however, as is clothing. And I noticed as we drove about the city that even at expensive-looking homes the clothes were hung out on lines to dry. Apparently few people have automatic clothes dryers. And many of the appliances that Americans take for granted did not seem to be on sale, at least where we looked.

As we drove about town I looked at the houses, noticing that all the roofs were a shade of reddish orange. Some of the roofs were tile, while the poorer homes had tin roofs, painted to resemble tile. Advertisements in the newspaper showed houses were selling for $A18,000 to $A30,000; these were homes of what were called fourteen to eighteen squares (I learned subsequently that a square is one hundred square feet).

Ads in the same newspaper showed that automobiles were far, far more expensive, but that salaries were not quite what Americans would expect. A secretary made about $A300 per month, a mill operator $A150 a week, and a live-in maid working a five and one-half-day workweek received $A45 per week. Schoolteachers locally got a starting salary of $A5,800 per year.

For our evening meal we drove out to a Colonel Sanders Kentucky Fried Chicken place we had observed, and there at an exorbitant price we ate a fried-chicken dinner, washing it down with Coca-Cola. The stuff was just as greasy in Australia as in Oklahoma or California, but apparently it was selling well in Australia for the red-and-white striped huts were everywhere, complete with a picture of the Colonel himself. Normally Laura does not like Kentucky Fried Chicken, but this she ate with gusto—whereupon I concluded that she was becoming a mite homesick.

Driving out to this place and then back to the motel made me think about the habits I had acquired over many years. The fabric of ourselves is woven from a thousand tiny threads, each of which individually is weak and easily broken. However, these threads, when woven together to make up an individual personality, are incredibly strong—a rope of steel —and they bind us to our culture and our religion and our lifestyle. We are so accustomed to these threads that we never think about how we perform many daily events; these are habit to us, and we are left free to drift through life with little effort.

Take, for example, the matter of driving. I got my driver's license when I was eighteen years old (right after I returned from Korea), and I have been driving without an accident— and only three tickets—for twenty-three years. The habits acquired in this quarter-century of driving are like steel hawsers. To be forced suddenly to change to driving on the left side of the road suddenly makes driving a chore again, much as it was during the first few months I tried to pilot a car down the road. At home I can breeze along in city traffic with no great effort; I can drive and carry on a conversation, laugh and joke with the children, point to a bargain here or there in a store window, and indicate an occasional something worth noting, all the while moving with the flow of traffic and obeying all the laws. In Hobart, though, just to drive down the street required one hundred and ten percent of my powers of concentration, and I angrily snapped at the children several times, telling them to behave when the real problem was not their behavior but my frustration at trying to drive on an unfamiliar side of the road in a strange city.

For those of you who have never tried driving on the left side of the road, this comparison may help you understand. Take some forty-year-old from an Iowa farm and thrust him suddenly onto the freeways of Los Angeles, and see how white his knuckles become. Every summer in Los Angeles you can see these people—the husband has a death grip on the steering wheel as he moves along at forty-five miles an hour, a menace to himself and to all other traffic, while his wife has her head buried in a map and tells him that to get to Disneyland they need to turn onto the Santa Ana Freeway. Naturally she speaks just five seconds after they have passed the offramp for the Santa Ana Freeway—and ten miles from some place where he can turn around. This is how I felt driving on the left side of the road in Tasmania, and every habit of my life screamed at me that everyone else suddenly had gone crazy.

It was just such things as this that made Laura and me understand why some Americans who had immigrated to Australia suddenly decided to return home. They were unable, in the language of our astronauts, to attain separation speed from their native culture.

In trying to carry on conversations with Australians, we found that we were readily understood. But we found that we had some difficulty understanding many of them. This must be, one of them suggested, because they were raised on American television and movies, and thereby American "English" was common to them, but their accent strange to us. At home I have heard people talking of moving to Australia, whereupon someone is certain to remark, "Well, at least they speak English there, and you won't have to learn a new language." It is true that we two, Americans and Australians, do speak the same words, but we do not speak the same language. There is a large difference between a collection of words and a language. Just as civilization as we have known it in the United States is made up of many things, our culture is more than the sum of its parts. An American pilot on an airliner will come on the intercom and say, "This is your captain speaking," or, "This is Captain Smith." But the Australian pilot says, "Captain here." The words are the same. The style is slightly different. But the import, the meaning of the words, is worlds apart.

Back at our motel we watched the "Mickey Mouse Club," a show that went off the air at home some fifteen years ago. Apparently American television shows, when they grow old, do not die—they immigrate. Looking through *TV-*

Radio Guide for Hobart, I located "Hogan's Heroes," "Laramie," "Bonanza," "Lucy," and a dozen more, even "Lassie" and some shows so obscure that I never saw more than one or two of them at home. However, there may be some Americans pleased to know that in Hobart, Tasmania, Annette Funicello is still a teenager—and apparently will remain one forever as she serenades Mickey Mouse.

When before retiring we filled out our preferences for breakfast, we confronted something new: "Vegemite." This was printed there alongside spaghetti on toast, grilled tomatoes, and other traditional Australian breakfast items. I was so curious about what Vegemite might prove to be that I asked the lady at "reception" about it. She was shocked. "You don't have Vegemite in the United States?" she asked, both sympathy and shock in her voice. I subsequently learned that Vegemite, a product made by Kraft Cheese Company, is some kind of beef extract made into a paste. Australians spread this on toast and ate it with gusto. However, to me the taste was like cold beef broth while the smell seemed to come from some long-dead outhouse.

The next morning we set out to see the sights, driving to the top of Mt. Wellington for a sublime view of the Derwent Estuary and the city below. As we drove, I noted that the people working on Tasmania's roads, the construction crews, seemed about as busy as comparable workers at home—which is to say they were doing almost nothing. For years I have with astonishment watched huge numbers of these laborers take from eighteen to twenty-four months to complete even the smallest stretch of two-lane road, and every day as I pass their place of toil three-quarters of the workers are doing absolutely nothing. The same holds true in Tasmania, so I suppose this is a worldwide trait of road workers. There must be some fraternity for these people to teach them to do nothing all day—and then go home to complain to their wives about what a hard day they have had.

The western portion of Tasmania, that part directly to

the west and northwest of Hobart, is a haven for rugged individualists who really want to rough it. The mountains are jagged and jumbled beyond belief, the roads for the most part still dirt tracks, and the population more scant than it was twenty years ago. In fact, some parts are so remote that they have as yet not been fully explored. A fellow in Hobart fell to telling me about places to the west where there are sudden deep ravines, but that the trees growing up out of these are similar to an umbrella, and their branches form a solid cover over the ravines. The unwary person walking along on safe ground suddenly will walk out on these branches and fall through to the ravine below—and not be found again. This sounded like some wild story for tenderfeet, but I later found the same story in official literature. This is the kind of place you might recommend to someone really looking to get away from it all—like the type of person who would move to Alaska.

While Laura and the children shopped in and around Cat and Fiddle Square, which was the focal point of a huge downtown shopping complex much like our own malls, I began talking with people sitting around. Word quickly spread that I was a Yank, and soon I found myself talking with a couple of American immigrants. Both had come on assisted immigration, meaning the government had paid part of their passage fare. Neither was happy. The island state simply was too different from what they had known at home; in fact, most Australians readily claim that it is the most British part of Australia (and not a few will tell you that it is like the England of a quarter-century ago). Both of these fellows said they were making less money than they had at home, although they had believed their salaries would be comparable. One was a lorry (truck) driver and the other a heavy machinery operator, and both were unhappy with the lower standard of living to which they had been forced to adjust in Australia.

"I'd go home if I had the money," one said.

The other nodded, adding, "The worst part is that so few Americans move to Tasmania, and I get lonesome." Just then a third former American walked up, whereupon the first two quickly excused themselves and left. I was not left wondering why two men lonesome for talk of home left one of their own; this new fellow quickly proved to be the type that gives the United States a bad name. Not that he had retained his citizenship or that he bragged about the United States—no, that was not his problem. In fact, it was just the opposite. He was a "New Australian," as immigrants are called, one who could remember nothing good about the nation that gave him birth and nurtured him through his first two and one-half decades. He did not really want to talk to me, only to quarrel. Right off he told me that the quality of life in Australia was infinitely superior to that in America and that the United States was bound to ruination because of crime, drugs, political assassinations, corruption, student riots, and economic uncertainty. He declaimed at length about organized crime in the States and how these criminals were supplying Americans with booze, girls, gambling, loans, drugs, protection, business favors, and union cooperation and that all this made possible the payment of $20,000,000,000 a year in graft money to politicians in return for immunity from prosecution. I had not heard of such as this man told since last I saw some of the late-night movies about Al Capone.

I replied that indeed we had problems at home, but that I had been reading in Australian newspapers that the Mafia was moving into the Land Down Under. Immediately this chap fell to ranting against politics and politicians along with the loose moral climate in his new home.

"Did you know," he thundered, "that there actually are prostitutes in Sydney?" he asked me.

I allowed as how I did not know this fact for a certainty, and wondered how he had come to learn it. All the while I tried to keep a straight face, for I remembered reading about the reasons that so many of the original female convicts had been sent to Botany Bay back in 1788 to found the city of Sydney. This fellow was just warming up about the galloping sins that had come to Australia. He told me that now there was illegal gambling in Australia, another of the sins that the founding fathers of the nation would recognize; and he said that at the legal casino (referring, no doubt, to Wrest Point in Hobart) there was skimming of money before taxes were paid. "The police evidently are being paid off," he informed me with a knowing look.

We talked awhile more, and then I saw my family returning. His parting shot was, "Can Australia afford to exchange its high quality of life for the American paranoia?"

This fellow was becoming more and more like some character created by Lewis Carroll. "What do you recommend should be done to prevent that from happening?" I asked him.

"Why we've got to have informed, conscientious citizens, and we have to hold our politicians accountable," he thundered, causing several passersby to stare at us. "Corruption is just like war crimes; you either fight it, or else you're guilty through complacency."

This conversation was so good that I immediately wrote it in the pocket notebook I was keeping. Laura and the children wanted to know why I was laughing when they joined me. I told them I had been entertained by a kook looking for some soapbox on which to stand.

They had bought Richard a jacket and Nancy a purse, and both showed me their purchases. Then we went to Myers for lunch, after which we went down to look at Parliament House. There a half-asleep guard told us that visitors were permitted only by appointment, so we wandered down to the harbor to see the many oceangoing vessels loading or unloading there. Afterward we drove out to the Queen's Domain—a fancy name for the city park that overlooks the Tasman Bridge (built at a cost of $14,000,000, a plaque tells us). There over a pot of tea and some "sweets," as Australians call the many pastries for sale at every tea counter, we discussed our impressions of Tasmania.

Laura noted that in Australia the people walk on the left side of the sidewalk, just as they drive on the left side of the road. "Even their escalators work the reverse of ours," she commented. "The one on the left is the one going up."

"And we had to pay three cents to go into the ladies' restroom," Nancy commented. This reminded me of something we had read in one of the guidebooks; traditionally in Australia the ladies have been charged to use public restrooms. "Spend a penny" was slang among the local females for going to the restroom, but inflation had driven the cost of even this necessity to three cents.

"Well, the men's room is still free," Richard told them. "But I can't find a water fountain anywhere."

"At least we didn't have to pay any sales tax," Laura concluded. In thinking about this, we remembered that we had not been charged a sales tax in Sydney, Melbourne, and Launceston. Apparently they have not yet learned of this invention or their politicians would have adopted it; from what we have read, the taxes in Australia apparently are horrendously high. The income tax rapidly rises to fifty percent on everything above $A20,000, but we have read that there is no tax on capital gains.

Going back to our motel room, one other thought occurred to us. "The doors don't have doorknobs. Have you noticed this?" Laura asked. The children and I looked, and she was right. Most of the doors have a keyhole and a slender handle that is shoved down, but no doorknob.

That evening I asked what everyone wanted to eat. Laura again suggested Colonel Sanders, and the children agreed with her. Now I know my family is a victim of those endless television commercials at home that imply that eating the Colonel's chicken is more fun than seeing a circus, but Laura really does not like it. Her choice of this made me conclude that she might not be just homesick but that perhaps it was something more serious.

I was right. That evening as we watched television and saw Superman catch crooks twenty years ago despite the ravages of Kryptonite, I noted that Laura looked ill. Such was the case. She had a fever and was feeling bad. We previously had decided to drive up the Lake Highway to Great Lake in the center of the island, and then we were going to follow the Poatina Highway to Launceston; from there we would go west on Bass Highway to Devonport, there to catch the overnight boat to Melbourne. However, this trip, which we intended to begin the next day, would take us to places where doctors—good ones—were difficult to find. At Laura's insistence, we postponed any decision until the following morning to see if she had improved.

At breakfast on that last day of May, I saw Laura quietly taking aspirin and knew that she was not feeling well. Nor was that breakfast likely to make her feel better. With our toast that morning we had "leatherwood honey," one of the four flavors of honey for which the island reportedly is famous. The proprietor told us, when we inquired, that this result of the leatherwood tree nectar is greatly appreciated by the Japanese and that great quantities of the honey are exported to Japan. To me it tasted like soap, and a not very high quality soap at that. I could not eat it, nor could the children or Laura.

Because Laura's fever would not abate and because we felt we might have need of a good doctor, we dropped in at the state travel agency, sold our tickets on the overnight ship, and purchased air tickets to Melbourne. Sitting there at the airport, I read the morning paper and learned that the prime minister of Australia, Mr. Whitlam, wanted his Parliament to give him authority to exercise wage-and-price controls in order to halt inflation. I thought to myself about what had happened three years ago in the United States, where wage-and-price controls had failed so miserably to halt inflation. All they had done to me was prevent my getting a raise for a year.

By the time we turned the car in, checked our bags, and had our boarding passes, it was tea time, or so our children pointed out. Tea time was something they readily accepted, especially since they—and all Australians—ate quantities of pastries. At the snackbar in the airport, I noticed that among the other goodies for sale were tomato sandwiches, something I regard as quite unusual. These were sandwiches consisting of two slices of bread heavily buttered, between which were thin slices of tomatoes. That was all. These were priced exactly the same as roast beef sandwiches. Perhaps tomatoes were a delicacy here in the fall.

At last our flight was called aboard Ansett and we crossed the "tarmac," as they call it, to board. As the plane lifted into a cloudless sky and we gazed back at this beautiful island, we talked about the things there that had impressed us. All of us agreed that this island of apple orchards and sheep grazing in pastures and golf courses was absolutely lovely, and that its cities were beautiful. Everywhere the lawns and homes were particularly well kept, and we saw no slums. Some of the homes were extremely old, and some were very small, but all were painted and clean, with no litter about. Apparently slums are created first in the minds of people (despite all the counterclaims by sociologists); they do not come from the physical age of the buildings. Mental laziness precedes physical deterioration. There would be no slums in the United States if the people living in them wanted to keep them neat and clean. And at almost every house there were extensive flower beds rioting with color. And we decided that Tasmanians love the game of golf, for the courses were everywhere.

Also, we were fascinated by the number of children wearing school uniforms. Richard and Nancy were particularly impressed with this, as they were by the practice of separating the sexes in the grades. Moreover, we noticed that schooling ends at an early age for most Australians; education ends at age fifteen in every state except Tasmania, where it extends to age sixteen. Thereafter most teenagers begin working. We saw dozens of clerks in the stores who could have been little beyond the age of sixteen. Only a very few go on to college (which is their name for prep school) and the universities. Most of those who do have this opportunity are graduates of what we would call private schools, not of the public schools. The private schools educate their children almost exclusively to take the college boards (or whatever is the Australian name for what we call the college boards).

In Launceston we had inquired about this practice of wearing school uniforms, which must be quite expensive. Every school has its own colors, and therefore we knew that a parent would have to buy these all over again should his child move from one school to another. We were told that the cost annually came to more than a hundred dollars Australian, but that each school ran a thriftshop where used uniforms were sold. Remembering my own childhood, I can imagine how the other children would make life miserable for the student wearing used uniforms. Children can be terribly cruel, just as can snobbish parents who continue to vote for the wearing of uniforms.

On this airplane the coffee continued bad, very bad. No wonder every Australian I have seen ordering coffee asked for it "white" (with cream). And everything you ordered (or which you got complimentary on the airplane) had butter on it. Our sweet roll here had a pat of butter on it, as had the steaks I had ordered at several places; the steaks would come from the kitchen with a pat of butter sitting in the middle melting. In addition, the milk in Tasmania tasted funny. This, no doubt, was from the gum-tree flavor that permeated the water. Come to think of it, I had seen no Australian adult drinking milk.

And every adult Australian, it seemed, smoked like a furnace. On the television the Marlboro commercials were still booming out the song that makes the hair stand up on the back of the neck, while local brands tried to convince you that the way to prevent bad breath, improve your love life, and bring about a pay raise was to smoke this or that brand. Somehow it was almost comforting to know that the Marlboro man had not been put out of a job by the surgeon general's report. But as we flew across Bass Strait that last day of May—two weeks after I had ceased to smoke—my concern was not about my desire to light up, but about the state of my wife's health.

IV.

Victoria and South Australia

FROM THE AIR the visitor can see how Melbourne spreads itself around Port Phillip Bay, an urban sprawl that rivals Los Angeles. Moreover, as we drove from the new airport into town over the freeway, the bright sunlight, the waving palm trees, and the wide streets with their mercury-vapor lamps reinforced the comparison. Melbourne at first glance looked a great deal like Los Angeles.

However, we quickly discerned that the similarities are only skin-deep, for Melbourne has its own peculiar and distinct identity. True the city was cold in the early mornings of autumn when we were there, and the fog moved in to lend a touch of gray to the beginning of each day. But Melbourne is a city of bookstores and restaurants, of theaters and hotels, of art galleries and museums, along with splashy green parks, racetracks, and playing fields. And there are sections of town dominated by immigrants, the New Australians, where pizza is more easily purchased than fish and chips.

But Melbourne also struck me as a city living on past memories and past glories—somewhat in the way Tennessee Williams pictures the old-line Southern aristocrats: decadent, but with a baroque mellowness about them. Everywhere in Melbourne there is beauty, but it all looks as if it were built about 1935. For some reason I kept thinking of Fort Worth, although Melbourne, with its 2,500,000 citizens, is far larger. Fort Worth is a city that really has not grown a great deal in the past twenty years, where the architecture and the styles look as if they have not changed for a generation. Melbourne likes to advertise itself as the financial capital of the nation and the headquarters for all the major corporations. I could believe these ads, for most of the people looked as if they had spent their lives cooped up in some countinghouse. Melbourne was the site of the 1956 Olympics, and here the Melbourne Cup is run, an annual horse race that brings the nation to a standstill to listen and bet and cheer. But the local men have that pallor that comes from staying indoors too much. And they dress with the properness of Britishers who take themselves a little too seriously.

At the airport we checked out a car from Avis—and discovered the Holden. In 1948 General Motors began assembling this automobile here, the first car to be made in Australia. Now Ford assembles the Falcon here, Chrysler makes one of its cars here, and one of the British manufacturers assembles a car here. But General Motors was first, and Australians apparently remember, for the Holden is still the largest-selling car on the continent. I had hoped for something unique, but I found the Holden to be a Chevrolet Nova—with a left-hand drive, of course. However, it did not drive as easily as a Chevrolet at home; the steering ratio was different, and it had that stiffness about it that marks a car not well made. I almost fainted later when I learned that the Holden sells for more than $A5,000 (or $7,500 American).

As we drove into town we noted that the roofs here likewise were of tin or tile, and all a reddish orange. Our motel here was called the Caravilla, which is part of the TraveLodge chain. Neither it nor any other motel we had stayed in provided washcloths (here they call these "face washes"). And the water in Melbourne still tasted like the gum-tree smell. Laura called the American consul and asked for the names of some doctors; she then called one of them and made an appointment for tomorrow. Her fever was such that we spent the rest of the day in the room reading, relaxing, and talking about our impressions of this country.

Apparently Australian eating habits are not exactly like those of Americans. By this I mean that we have found expensive restaurants catering to the wealthy and to tourists, and there are motel and hotel restaurants where travelers eat. All of these advertise themselves as "licensed," which means that they are authorized by the government to sell liquor. But there seem to be almost no restaurants where food is available at reasonable prices in the evenings—nothing comparable to our quick-food places except the ubiquitous Colonel Sanders' Kentucky Fried Chicken places and McDonald's hamburger stands. Everywhere here and in Tasmania there were "Take Out Food" shops; these are a kind of grill or even a delicatessen, but with no sit-down facilities. You buy your food and take it out somewhere to eat. And there are "Milk Bars," which sell sandwiches and "sweets" (a combination of cookies, doughnuts, pies, and pastries). But there seem to be almost no inexpensive restaurants with dine-in facilities and not serving liquor.

We had with us on this trip one of the guidebooks to the South Pacific, one which supposedly would tell us where to go and what to see and would save us from being gypped. We found it wrong more often than right. The authors of these things, from what I could tell, act like jet-setters, staying in the best hotels and eating in the best restaurants—and recommending both to the casual visitor on a limited budget. The authors must do this because they get many things free or at reduced rates in return for mentioning the establishment in their books. The average tourist will find these things useless. If you do go into the restaurants mentioned in one of the guides to the city, you most probably will find few local citizens there, just other tourists like yourself—and all of you wondering where the people from Melbourne eat.

And there apparently is no such thing as "Australian" cooking. I guess every American has dined at an Italian restaurant or a Mexican restaurant or perhaps a German restaurant. Well, an Australian restaurant would have a blank menu, for there are no Australian dishes. Basically what they eat is English in origin. I was told by one restaurant owner that there have been attempts to create or manufacture something Australian, out of some sense of local pride and to seek some national identity. One hustler did begin to can— for export—kangaroo tail soup; the local citizens were smart enough to stay away from it. I remember seeing rattlesnake stew advertised in Arizona, but I do not recall any Arizonans eating it; such must be the case with this kangaroo tail soup. I also was told that over in Adelaide they had invented the "pie floater," which is a kind of meat pie; some Australians claimed this was "real Australian cooking." I looked forward to trying it.

Most Australians with whom I discussed food seemed to recognize that there is no national dish, and they made jokes about it. Inasmuch as I heard the following from several people, it must be a standard tale for tourists. According to this story, Australian cooking falls into three categories: first, bush damper, which is slang for food to be eaten in the Outback; the recipe for this is, mix flour and water, then cook. Second, witchetty grubs, meaning what the aborigines eat; the recipe is, catch anything that moves, do not cook, do not kill, just eat. And third, cockatoo stew, the recipe for which is, boil a cockatoo in water with an old boot, and when cooked, throw away the cockatoo and eat the boot.

When you go into an Australian restaurant, what you will find on the menus is prime beef, which will be prepared as you would expect: fried, roasted, and baked, all in the same way as in any Hilton or Sheraton Hotel or Holiday Inn anywhere. There will be fish in its various forms, particularly shrimp (which they call "prawns"); ham—and a favorite here is "Ham Hawaiian," which means it will be smothered in pineapple; and mutton. Once while we were in Melbourne I accidentally got a piece of mutton off a buffet. I actually had a piece of the stuff in my mouth and was chewing on it when I realized what it was; awareness dawned on me when the thing began to swell the more I chewed it. It may be my Texas origins that makes me say it, but I have always maintained that a person has to be a little degenerate to like mutton.

Tonight's paper—and the motels here furnish the paper free—reveals much of the cause of Melbourne's urban sprawl. Apparently every Australian, like his American cousin, dreams of owning his own home set on his own eighty-by-one-hundred-twenty-foot lot. And Melbourne definitely is a town of urban sprawl along with urban blight and urban pollution. The newspapers are full of all the current catchwords about the ecology and the environment and the need to protect both. There are even a host of federal laws relating to the environment and protecting it from pollution—apparently with about the same success as Los Angeles has had on this score.

According to the paper the Australian who wants to buy even minimum housing needs a savings of $5,500 in order to get a loan. There is a ceiling of $15,000 on loans for housing, and the average minimum cost of a house in Melbourne has now grown (should I say inflated) to $20,500. Moreover, interest rates on loans for homes have gone out of sight. Tonight's newspaper carries many ads asking to borrow money and offering to pay eleven and even twelve percent interest. The home that cost an average $16,000 in January 1974 has risen to $20,500 by the summer of the same year, and the interest rates on home loans through federal sources is ten and three-quarter percent. But according to this paper the average wage has not kept pace with inflation. The highest average weekly wage, $A120.90, is in the state of Victoria (which, of course, means Melbourne); the lowest weekly wage, $A110.00, is in Tasmania. Considering these wages and the price of housing, I can understand why we have yet to see any slums; no one can afford to allow his house to run down.

Richard and Nancy both have noticed that the Australians have a curious way of phrasing things. Nancy was reading the paper tonight and pointed out a phrase, "When many patrons nominate the same time. . . ." She asked what it meant. I read that section of the paper a couple of times before I understood that it meant, "When many patrons choose (or select) the same time. . . ."

While Nancy and I were discussing this, Richard pointed out that I should put in my notes that the toilets here are strange. The seats are extremely flimsy, and the water tanks are not immediately behind and connected to the toilets themselves. Rather the tanks are separate and raised almost to eye level behind the toilets. And the flushing mechanism is activated not by a lever in the upper lefthand corner, as in the United States, but by a button usually located in the middle of the tank itself (but occasionally up on top of the tank).

The next morning after we ate the breakfast delivered to our room, we drove around the town to familiarize ourselves with it. Laura's fever temporarily had gone down—naturally it would just before she went to the doctor. As we drove through the downtown section and around the waterfront, we noted that nowhere had we seen any hippies. Any of the young over here who might be inclined to go out seeking to "discover themselves" instead found that they must go to work. Everywhere in the stores we saw clerks who were only fifteen or sixteen years old. I do think it would be fitting for all the hippies of the world to be reincarnated in Australia—as sheep; this would be a hippie's version of heaven, for all a sheep has to do is eat and grow hair.

As we drove about Melbourne—and we were downtown and in the botanical gardens—I saw the English desire for a piece of land leading to urban sprawl. It seemed to take forever to drive across this town. Yet in the St. Kilda area, it looked like some ethnic section of New York City or Chicago, for the streets were filled with Italian and Greek immigrants. Melbourne had more land set aside as parks than comparable American cities; the early governors must have been the ones to insist on this, I knew, for no contemporary politician, Australian or American, would possess such wisdom.

And everywhere in Melbourne, as in Tasmania, there were travel agencies. One of the favorite places apparently—for posters everywhere urged visitors to go there—is Tasmania. "Your Vacation Isle" and "Little Tassie" were the names applied. Apparently Australians look on Tasmania as a place for honeymooning and for vacations, a kind of Niagara Falls. From what we had seen so far of Sydney and Melbourne, we had to agree that Tasmania was different from the rest of Australia.

Just after lunch we searched our city map again and found on it the location of the doctor's office where Laura was to go. Finding the office itself proved a little more difficult, but eventually we arrived there. Just beside his office was a small park, and I waited with the children there, allowing them to play with some young Australians, while Laura went inside. Just as we both had surmised, she had some kind of staph infection from that shot in Fiji; for this the doctor prescribed an antibiotic. This prescription cost just $A1.00 to have filled at a nearby drugstore, a cost that seemed most reasonable to Americans accustomed to paying ten to fifteen dollars for something similar at home.

Afterward, while Laura rested in the motel and the children played in yet another park, one near the motel, I visited the Australian-American Association and Club. This is located on the fifth floor at Sixty Collins Street. Soon I found myself talking with Americans recently moved to Australia, for I was more interested in their comments than in those of Australians interested in the United States.

To my question, "Why did you move to Australia?" the most common answer, one we would hear time and again as we traveled through the country, was, "I wanted a better place to raise my children."

In this group with whom I was talking were three former Americans and one American businessman who had no thought of changing his citizenship. "Family life is important here, more so than in the States," said one of the immigrants, a fellow who had moved here from San Francisco. "My wife and our children go sailing and camping together, something we never did at home." I wondered why it was easier to go sailing together here than it was back in San Francisco, so I asked him. "Somehow it seems we have more of an interest in doing things together here," he answered weakly.

In the back of my mind there began the glimmering of an idea that later would grow stronger: many of the people who have immigrated to Australia could have had the same thing without moving, if they had been willing to take the time or if they had been sufficiently interested.

A second of the immigrants, this one from Chicago, spoke up: "The schools here give a better education," he thought. "My children are forced to work harder in school, and because the schools are not coeducational they concentrate more and study harder."

The third immigrant, a stocky fellow from Indianapolis, agreed: "My children study more here because they don't watch television as much. People here aren't as preoccupied with TV. In fact, people here can still actually carry on a conversation."

"I got tired of newscasters screaming 'crisis' at me every evening," the second fellow said. "Here I don't get that from the newscasters on TV. They are more subdued in that British sort of way. And, frankly, I don't watch the news as regularly as I did back home."

Listening to this kind of talk made me wonder why he didn't stay home, and leave the TV turned off there. But the first fellow agreed with him, at least in a lefthanded sort of way: "I wanted to move someplace not so materialistic as the United States. And Aussies aren't as materialistic as Americans. They want more time off from their jobs to be with their families."

This fellow might have more time off, I thought, but he certainly did not seem to be taking it with his family. Rather he was coming down to this club to talk with fellow (former) Americans, seemingly to reinforce his own belief in the correctness of the action he had taken. The third member of that group spoke up again. "Food here is cheap," he allowed, "and we camp out a lot, my family and me. In the United States when we went on vacation we thought we had to stay in first-class motels. But here we don't. We camp out, and it costs a lot less." I couldn't help thinking of the thousands of Americans who camp out on their vacations, and wondered why this fellow thought he had to stay in a motel.

I turned to the businessman who had not immigrated and asked his opinions and impressions about Australia. "This is a man's country," he told me. "It's not a woman's country as it is back in the States. And this not only is a man's country, it's a workingman's country. To get along here you have to go along easily not asking too much of life financially and materially."

"It sounds to me like you're poor-mouthing it," I said to him, for he was dressed in a way that implied he was getting a great amount of financial and material benefit out of life.

"Well," he replied with a smile, "it's not too popular over here for an American to say he's making money in the country, so I just tell everyone that this is a workingman's country —which, of course, it isn't. And I tell them that the reward of working here is the happiness of being in a man's country. Yep," he concluded, "I poor-mouth it, as you say."

Is there much hatred of Americans, I wanted to know. "Some," said the businessman, "especially if they think you're making money over here."

The immigrant from Chicago offered yet another viewpoint. "Some Americans come over here and rent a house," he said. "Then they find it, as well as the apartments here, doesn't have the appliances they have at home—a dishwasher, a washing machine, a clothes dryer. And the wife begins complaining. Soon the husband gets unhappy because his wife is unhappy, and both begin whining that America is better than Australia. Aussies don't like to hear that kind of talk. So they don't talk to this kind of immigrant, and they get lonely and unhappy and soon they go home. But usually the Aussies like most Americans, especially those that make some effort to get along."

"By that," the businessman told me, "he means the Aussies like those Americans who complain just a little about the States, but not too much. Aussies don't like a whiner, but neither do they like a braggart. So if you get along, like I said earlier, you'll find friends easy enough. The Aussies really are a pretty good bunch. And they do have some of the best beer in the world." He took a deep drink to prove his point.

The talk swirled about for a couple of hours, but most of what I heard was summed up in the words of one of the immigrants: "Living costs are much higher here than I had thought they would be. A car, a refrigerator, a television set—all cost as much, if not more, than they did in American dollars at home, and that doesn't take into account the difference in the value of the two currencies. Generally you earn about one-third less here than in the States—which is about an equal amount of money when you switch currencies—but you can't live as well here on that as you can at home.

"So many things are imported that living in Australia is really expensive. If when you arrive here you can pay cash for your house, your furniture, and your car, you can live quite well on a small amount of money."

I did not say anything, but my thought was that you can live quite well on very little *anywhere* if you own your house, car, and furniture.

After I left this club, I returned to the motel and for a time watched Richard and Nancy as they played with the Australian children in the park. The children here, at least those in

Melbourne, seemed just as noisy and boisterous as their American counterparts—until they reach the age of thirteen or fourteen; then somehow they become better behaved and quieter (at least around adults).

That evening, as we watched television, Laura and I talked for a time about what we had seen so far and what we felt. We concluded that travel really was not "broadening," as the cliché states it. Rather, we believed, travel merely reinforces preexisting prejudices. Those who love the United States come to appreciate it all the more when they travel, while those who hate their home find other places to be great, faulting their home by comparison.

The next morning, Sunday, I read in the newspaper of some effort under way to promote "made in Australia" and "buy Australian," followed by some of what at one time was called "English and proud of it." In short, the Aussies seemed to be deliberately promoting a national consciousness, close behind which comes an awareness of their British traditions. However, the Japanese influence is obvious, and the American influence is almost overpowering.

In the same newspaper was an article stating that, according to a recent study, one out of every six Australian schoolchildren read so poorly as to need remedial help immediately. This was not new, for I remembered seeing similar studies in the United States. The paper also contained stories about labor unrest during the severe inflation haunting the nation that summer of 1974. And Australian authors, according to the paper, were suing to collect royalties on their materials that were Xeroxed! I knew firsthand that American authors were losing much money they would gain from sales because of illegal copying. Come to think of it, I read nothing in the local newspapers that convinced me Australians have fewer problems than we do at home; in fact, their problems are no different at all.

And, finally, I noticed from the same paper that automobiles are fantastically expensive. A Pontiac Firebird Trans-Am was listed for sale at only $A14,500, while a 1972 Chevrolet Camaro with 9,000 miles of experience was advertised as a real bargain at $A5,750.

There was not much available for us to do that day, for almost everything closes in Australia on Sunday, No one here seems to want—or even is willing—to work on Saturday afternoon or Sunday. There is a kind of "union" and "employee" mentality at work in the nation that prevents anyone from working too hard for anything. With some difficulty we did, as we drove around, at last find a takeout food store selling sandwiches. Richard ordered a hamburger, whereupon the girl at the counter asked if he wanted "the lot."

He turned to me and asked, "What's 'the lot'?"

I shrugged my shoulders in ignorance of what "the lot" might be. Richard proved adventuresome and told her that he would indeed take the lot. This proved to mean that the hamburger had onions, lettuce, and tomato on it—as well as two slices of bacon and a fried egg. Their concept of what constituted a hamburger astonished all of us, but Richard pronounced it "very tasty." This was the same eating establishment whose sign proudly proclaimed, "American Hamburgers Here."

That afternoon we walked through the zoo until Laura became tired. She and I then sat down in the tea shop while Richard and Nancy continued their tour. When I suggested to the waitress that a glass of water should accompany my spot of tea, a couple sitting at the next table turned and said, "You're Americans." This really was not a question or even a flat statement of fact, but rather a comment—and one loaded with friendliness.

We allowed as how this was a correct assessment, whereupon the woman wanted to know what state we were from. Told Oklahoma, she responded that she and her husband hailed from St. Louis originally. They had been in Australia seven years, and were not extremely happy.

"It's far more unionized than I thought," the man commented. "I came here as a pharmacist, but there are too many pharmacies and their trade union has made it difficult to get a license. I couldn't practice my trade here, so I had to find something else. Those who have the licenses still don't want competition."

"Some Americans come here with enough money to buy land and a house and a boat," said his wife, "and they love Australia. But don't come here and try to start from scratch. This can be hard country to accumulate things unless you are willing to work double or triple shifts at some manufacturing plant."

"Yep," sighed the man wearily, "and then the government takes most of what you make in taxes. The income tax here is terrible."

Laura changed the subject by asking what they thought was the best part of living in Australia.

"A day here is pretty much like the day before," said the man. Seeing our look of confusion, he continued, "I really like the fact that there's not a terrible lot of excitement. We don't get that sense of crisis that we had at home every evening on the television and every morning in the newspaper. We're satisfied and we're going to stay. Lots of Americans we've known who've come over have gone home because they get bored. But not us."

His wife nodded. "Teachers here are better than at home," was her comment. "Over here they take an interest in our children. It's not just a nine-to-three job with them like it was back home. Here they even welcome our children over to visit them at home on Saturdays."

The man continued, "At home I was on an economic treadmill. I owned my own pharmacy, but I found myself working nights and weekends to keep up with the payments on all the things we thought we had to have: a house, two cars, two television sets—color, naturally—and clothes. We lived in the right neighborhood, and I bought memberships in a good country club. Here we only have one car, a used Austin, and our house is old. I go to a public golf course and pay green fees. The kids swim at a public beach, not at the country-club swimming pool. And we seem to have time and money for everything we want. We aren't trying to keep up with the Joneses or anyone anymore."

Later during the conversation this couple let slip that they were keeping their American citizenship. I asked why. "Because," said the fellow, "I want my children to have the option of going there to live if they want to. And they probably will. All the young Aussies seem to think Los Angeles would be *the* place to be."

The next day, Monday, we set out driving westward toward Ballarat, just seventy-five miles away. For part of the distance the road was freeway, but all too soon it closed in and became a two-lane stretch very similar to my memories of U.S. 80 or U.S. 66 of twenty-five years ago. The countryside reminded me of western Kansas, say, the stretch from Abilene to Hays, or of parts of the Panhandle of Texas—or even (shades of LBJ) of the Hill Country of South Texas. What I am trying to say is that this was rolling country with few trees, a country of farming and grazing. However, off in the distance we occasionally could see something the road signs called mountains, but such rose only about two thousand feet or so and thus were little more than good-sized hills. And what trees were growing were of the gum variety and thus strange to the eyes of Americans.

We had lunch in a good restaurant in Ballarat, one connected with our motel. I guess the way to say it was a "good" restaurant is to note that it was "licensed." In Australia a "licensed" restaurant is one that can sell alcoholic beverages; usually these are very good. The milk for the children was delivered in glass bottles (although we had seen paper cartons). I guess what I am trying to point out here is that the plastic society had not yet fully arrived in Australia. Even the water and soft drinks on airplanes were not served in those abominable clear plastic "glasses," but in genuine glasses; and the coffee and tea were served in china cups. Nancy complained that the milk tasted funny, so I tried a sip. It did taste funny, because it was not homogenized. And I noticed that the cream visibly had risen to the top in the glass bottle.

For years I have sat around with others of my age and older and reminisced, "Remember when milk came in glass bottles and you could see the cream at the top." The thrust of such conversation is that the good old days were better. Well, that milk tasted strange. I am so accustomed to what we get today that I really did not like the rich taste of the cream. I guess I am part of the homogenized society, the one accustomed to drinking out of plastic "glasses."

After lunch we drove out to Sovereign Hill in Ballarat. This is the spot where gold was discovered in 1851 and where, three years later, the miners revolted against the British crown; this protest, which took place at Eureka Stockade, was against the license fees extracted from miners by the royal government. The miners banded together, raised their five-star flag, and proclaimed a republic. Americans who were there lustily joined this revolt, organizing themselves as the "Independent Californian Rangers Revolver Brigade" under the leadership of James McGill—who was only twenty-one years old. On December 3, British troops stormed the stockade, bayoneting the wounded and setting fire to the tents. McGill dressed himself as a woman and slipped away to Melbourne. So ended the battle at Eureka Stockade.

At Sovereign Hill there is something in the nature of an amusement park. However, this does not describe the establishment correctly. There are no rides or sideshows, but they do charge admission: $1.20 for adults and 30¢ for children. Inside there are buildings in the style of 1854, and in these are employees practicing—and selling—the crafts of twelve decades ago. The children panned for gold, unsuccessfully, and had a big time. We then went inside a mine, going about a third of a mile underground, after which we watched how metal was shaped into pans in a foundry. For a token fee we purchased some of these as souvenirs.

Across town at Eureka Stockade we looked at the diorama depicting the events of 1854. The monument is incredible in that it manages somehow to honor both the miners, called

Diggers, and the troops; it states that the rebels fell "in the fight for freedom," while the police and soldiers fell "at the call of duty." Only a British grammarian could straddle the fence so nicely. The Diggers are Australian heroes, genuine ones fighting for freedom, but the country is very much aware of its British heritage, including the empire and the Queen.

In textbooks about the American West, we read about the toughs in San Francisco during the rush of Forty-Nine. These criminals were called "Sydney Ducks," for many of them had come over from Australia. Well, in Australia the talk was about the "California Rangers" and the violence they loosed in the Land Down Under.

Society in Australia is sufficiently far behind that, in some ways, it is ahead. For example, in Ballarat, a city of 60,002 (according to a sign at the edge of town), they still have a city bus system working. They do not have to worry about getting money to start a mass transit system to help clean up the environment, for the old mass transit system never died. In Melbourne the tram system still operates. I guess people did not get cars in such numbers as to kill the buses and trams —and now they are so far behind that they are ahead.

We were awakened the next morning by our breakfast being shoved through a small door, sort of like something one might have cut for a dog to enter and leave the house. This allowed our breakfast to be delivered without our having to get up to open the door. Afterward we departed westward, intending to drive to Adelaide some 370 miles away. Leaving the "Garden City," as Ballarat likes to describe itself, we passed through the "Arch of Victory" at the western end of town. Straddling the highway, the arch celebrates the victory of 1918.

On this trip the children kept hoping to see some genuine wild animals, but all we spotted during this drive was one emu. The countryside itself reminded us very much of the delta of eastern Louisiana and Arkansas, but with an occasional mountain thrusting up to 2,000 or 2,500 feet. They really are not much for mountains, but they do jump upward some 1,500 feet from the plains below, and thus they do stand out.

At Bordertown, which, as the name implies, is on the border between the states of Victoria and South Australia, we paused to purchase gasoline, and there we bought a road map. Coming from the States, we found this a surprise; in Australia road maps are not free at service stations. We found the maps at BP (British Petroleum) service stations to be excellent, but we had to pay twenty-five cents for them. We little realized that on our return to the States we would find free road maps yet another aspect of American society that is disappearing. In Bordertown we paused to eat lunch at a takeout food place. Again Richard asked for a hamburger with "the lot" on it, but was disappointed to find he did not get an egg with it. Nancy contented herself with a ham sandwich and a chocolate bar—the chocolate here is excellent.

The approach to Adelaide on the highway we were using is astonishing. Just a few miles outside town you are driving on a flat plain. Then the two-lane highway becomes winding and climbs slowly. This is the Mount Lofty Ranges. Suddenly the road begins a winding and tortuous descent to the city below. Adelaide sits on a small plain between the sea and the mountains.

Using the city map, which was printed on the back of our BP state map, we negotiated through city traffic just at rush hour in the evening to arrive at our motel. We found it priced at $A20 (or $30 American), though it had few of the comforts we expected in a room at this price. Again, we found the food in the restaurant there to be reasonably priced and quite excellent.

We thought for a time about going to a movie this evening and so we looked in the newspapers to see what was on. We found that the same shows were running here as in the States, but three to six months later. And the same arguments were heard here about pornography and the difficulty of defining what is morally wrong in a free society. One

American with whom I discussed this problem said that he moved to Australia in part to escape the "moral decay" in the United States; he did not want his children to be confronted with magazines and books containing pictures of nudes every time they stopped at a newsstand. However, I noticed more of these on the newsstands in Australia than at home. In fact, many of the covers on paperback books featured frontal nudity to the waist—in a way that would never be acceptable at home. Even *Deep Throat*, the porno movie, was playing in Adelaide.

And, according to the newspaper, a team from the University of Kentucky was in town playing basketball with local Australian teams. Basketball apparently is really sweeping this country, and professional teams are in the offing here. However, as the newspaper noted, the Australian problem is how to get good teams without hiring American blacks to play on them. They want good teams, but not at the expense of their racial inclinations.

The next morning found Laura still not feeling extremely well. Her fever would come and go. However, she felt well enough to drive around the city and look at it. We found it a city of old buildings of brick and bluestone (a local stone with a blue cast). The hotels, the old ones, are noteworthy for their balcony porches. In fact, much of the city is a kind of living museum of nineteenth-century architecture, but in the extremely modern section of downtown there are new buildings that look just like much of what can be seen at home. According to the talk we heard locally, however, the downtown section of the city is dying.

Adelaide was laid out in 1836 by a Colonel William Light. His dream was to surround the city entirely with large parks. Therefore, the physical limits of the town are small, as is the population. In 1920 the town had 40,000 inhabitants, but in the census of 1971 there were only 16,313. Just past the parks around the town are many communities (thus when the population of Adelaide is given, it usually is about 750,000). But the inner city is dying because factories and warehouses have been allowed to violate Colonel Light's plan of an open city where the industrial section was banished outside the inner area. Now, according to the paper, the city fathers have a plan to "conserve the best of the historic physical environment and further develop the physical city for new as well as old uses." Their plan is to restore the city to the point where at least 30,000 people live in it.

At lunch time we stopped downtown in Myers Department Store's cafeteria, and there we tried Adelaide's famed meat pies and chips. These were not bad—but really not very good either. In fact, this meat pie was very similar to the frozen meat pies (beef potpie, turkey potpie, chicken potpie) sold in supermarkets in the States. I guess the best indication I can give you about these potpies is to note how much catsup is poured on them by the local citizens (and here they call catsup "tomato sauce"). Richard and Nancy quickly adapted, and when they had chips (French fries) they spoke up and asked for "tomato sauce."

That afternoon we continued to look around, even doing some shopping for opal jewelry. Australia produces about ninety-five percent of the world's opals, many of them coming from Coober Pedy, some four hundred miles northwest of Adelaide. We had seen some opals for sale in jewelry stores in Melbourne, but had decided to wait until we got to Adelaide; we were hoping that opals would be less expensive here. At one place, the Opal Bar, we found the prices so low that we had our doubts about the quality; at another place we found the prices so high that we had no doubts whatsoever. In the end we purchased nothing.

Walking through the streets of the downtown area, we noted that there was something about the sunlight here that made it seem unusually bright. In this respect it reminded me of southern Arizona or southern California. And the sun was extremely high on the northern horizon, so much so that it was getting dark by five in the afternoon. The city itself reminded me of downtown Fort Worth or Dallas of twenty-five years ago; however, in the oldest sections it seemed quite foreign. Everywhere there was Victorian gingerbread—ornately carved woodwork around the edges of roofs and around windows.

After looking at the people downtown—and these people basically were of English descent—I at first concluded that they were somewhat uglier than Americans. However, I soon changed my mind. The truth is, these people use less makeup than do Americans, and the American mania for cleanliness is not so evident. Moreover, I think they tend to wear out their clothes rather than try to keep up with the dictates of fashion. The more I thought about all these things, the more I tended to agree that the Australians have the right idea, but accepting this situation would require some mental adjustment.

Another facet of Australia was revealed to us as we walked around the downtown area: Australians love to travel more than almost anyone else I have ever known. It seemed that almost every other business place downtown was a travel agency. Each of the Australian states maintains a string of travel bureaus (Tasmania had three or four of them in Adelaide), and these manage to pay for themselves through the commissions generated from selling tickets.

Some of the random observations we had about Adelaide as we talked that evening at dinner were: first, how few Australians we saw drinking milk. An American we encountered in the restaurant that evening stated that in his three and one-half years in the country he had rarely heard an Australian in a restaurant ask for milk. Perhaps this explains why the adults' teeth in this nation are so notoriously bad. More than one-third of all people past twenty-five years old have false teeth. Second, most of the women here do not shave their legs. I understand that this is the standard European practice. And, third, the stores downtown do not give away free paper sacks. Anyone shopping for almost anything must bring his own shopping bag. When you purchase something, the best you can get is for the clerk to wrap a piece of paper around it.

The next morning Laura's fever had returned to the extent that we called the American consul to get a recommendation for a doctor. His receptionist proved most courteous, and we were told to come in as soon as possible. While Laura was in his office, the children and I waited in a nearby park, running and playing tag together. Some of the elderly people sunning themselves in the park looked at me as if I must be crazy for running with the children, but we had fun. Traveling brings a family close together—so much so that nerves get frayed. And Richard and Nancy get impatient traveling in a car or sightseeing just as all children do. Moreover, they sometimes get unhappy that they are not in control of their lives the way Laura and I are. Thus I was glad we had the time together in the park, for it brought us closer together.

After Laura got out of the doctor's office, we stopped by the railroad depot to purchase roundtrip tickets from Adelaide to Perth. An economy-class ticket for the roundtrip was $103 (or $154.50 American). First-class tickets cost more, but as Perth was 1,500 miles away, we figured we needed the additional space that a compartment afforded. We would leave on the 12:30 train two days hence.

Back outside in the downtown area, I noticed one other thing: the young girls all were wearing micro-mini skirts and those shoes with the terribly high heels (the things called clogs). These went out of fashion at home a year ago, but here they were all the rage—and as ugly on Australian girls as on American girls. I was beginning to think that when some item of apparel or some television show was dropped in the United States, the merchants sent all their remaining stock overseas. Again we were reminded of how much the United States is the fashion leader for the rest of the world.

At lunch we ate in the "Piccadilly" (cafeteria) on the top floor of David Jones Department Store. Nancy ordered a milk shake and discovered that the thing was different in Australia. It contained milk and a little flavoring mixed together in a milk-shake container, then was beaten (or shaken) in a blender; there was no ice cream in it. Richard had another of his hamburgers, and this also was different. The bread was not a bun, as we know it, and the meat was ground more coarsely. Even the "tomato paste," which served for catsup, was different; it *was*, literally, tomato paste with a few spices in it.

All this led Laura and me to make some observations about the food we had been eating. A nation's cooking can never be duplicated exactly, and the things labeled "American" here were not really American. The sausage, as I noted our first day in Australia, was different, as were the salami and bologna. The ham had more fat in it. The beef was grass-fed, not grain-fed, and much tougher than we were accustomed to eating—although the flavor was excellent. The Corn Flakes were made by Kellogg, no doubt exactly like those in America. However, the milk you poured on them was different in taste, and the sugar more coarse—so even Corn Flakes tasted different as you ate them. The coffee had gotten so dreadfully worse as we moved through the country—I would have sworn at first that such was impossible—that we had almost totally given it up. And in restaurants we had been served very few vegetables cooked or fresh; about the only hot vegetable served universally here was chips.

However, there was an astonishing diversity in the pastries served. Everywhere at morning or afternoon tea, there were thirty, forty, even fifty different varieties of cakes, cookies, and pastries.

On a subject closely related to food, one American told me that he had settled in Adelaide when he moved here because this was the first place he had found where the water did not taste like the gum tree. However, we noticed that the water in Adelaide had a slightly brown color and tasted like chlorine. "It's like drinking in the swimming pool," was Nancy's comment.

That evening we ate at the Hilton Inn's smorgasbord, and sampled some of the local wine. The nearby Barossa Valley is famed for its wine, and even is beginning to export this to other nations. We found it excellent. Several Australians with whom we talked told us that they take their vacations in the Barossa Valley just so they can stock up on wine inexpensively and because some of it is made in such limited quantities that it is sold only locally. We paid $2.70 for a bottle that would have been at least six or seven dollars at home.

Words here had funny turns, but there was a logic to them when you pondered them carefully: "Parking bay" for roadside park; "Don't rubbish Australia" for don't litter; "lift" for elevator; and "petrol" for gasoline. All in all, Australia so far seemed strange to us in that indefinable way that said this was not home. However, we were liking it very much. It seemed a little like Canada and a little like New England.

The next morning we set out to drive to Cleland National Park. This meant retracing our path into town—back up into the Mount Lofty Ranges, for the national park is just at the top of these peaks. Parking the automobile, we went inside for a token fee. There at last Richard and Nancy were able to pet a koala bear, which the director of the park, a lady, held for us. She explained that the koala is a slow animal because the leaves of the eucalyptus tree, which is its sole diet, contains juice that is fermented; thus the little animal, which is about as big as a medium-sized dog, stays drunk its entire life. *Koala* itself is an aboriginal word meaning "no water"; the koala never drinks, extracting the liquid it needs from the leaves it consumes. It attacks nothing, lives in trees, and is, in turn, hunted by almost no one. For many years in the early part of the twentieth century, it was killed by Australians for its fur. Now, however, it is protected by law and is multiplying once again.

There at this park we also were able to walk into a large area closed in by wire screens where cockatoos, parakeets (which the Australians call "budgies"), and even kookaburras flew free. The kookaburra is known in Australia as "the laughing jackass" and with good reason, for his laugh is much like that of the burro. While we were in this cage, cockatoos flew over and landed on our shoulders. One of these beautiful white birds then asked Nancy, "Don't you want a drink?" while another contented itself with telling Richard "Hello."

Wandering free in this park were both red and gray kangaroos, while pelicans and black swans could be found at a small lake. Then Richard discovered the cages housing the dingoes, which are medium-sized dogs, some a kind of yellow in color, others brown. And near the front of the establishment, in an enclosure we had not investigated as we entered, we found the wombats; these seemed to be cousins of the rabbit, but about the size of a hog.

The wind was blowing, and it was a wet, cold, miserable day. Therefore, we took refuge in the restaurant-curio store all too soon. There we met a fellow American, one who asked if we had run into the "rich American" syndrome as yet. I asked what he meant. "All Americans traveling in this country are considered rich," he told me, whereupon I assured him that such was not our case. "That doesn't matter," he replied. "All Americans who come here, either permanently or temporarily, even those who are just here as tourists, are considered wealthy. In fact, the Aussies will treat you with some resentment because they think you are rich. But if they find out you are not, then they will look on you as a failure. I don't know which is worse."

During our drive back down to Adelaide, we noticed something different: safety ramps for runaway trucks. Every mile or two on this downhill strip of road, always at a place where the road curved to the right (for we were driving on the left side of the road), a dirt road would lead straight ahead from the point where the road curved—and it would run uphill. Thus the driver whose brakes failed could run his vehicle straight ahead onto one of these safety ramps, and he could bring it to a safe halt on this uphill grade. This seemed a very positive idea.

For lunch we paused at Colonel Sanders' place once again, but I am not certain why. It was greasy and overpriced: $1.60 for an individual portion. Why any Australian in his right mind would eat this is beyond me. To feed the four of us cost $7.31—we ate T-bone steak for less in Tasmania.

After lunch, while Laura rested and the children watched television, I went to the University of South Australia for a visit. There I visited with the head of the Department of History and with a couple of his professors. Strangely the man in charge of teaching American history seemed the most reluctant to talk with me, and he soon disappeared. Perhaps an American professor of history made him nervous. Very soon I was in the seminar room having a cup of tea with these people—who made me feel right at home; in fact, I had to remind myself visibly that I was in a foreign university. We spent a couple of hours discussing our respective problems and making comparisons. The major difference that I could see was that classes there ran late into the afternoon. The department head explained that his professors had many classes for students who were government clerks for the state and who could take courses only late in the afternoon or at night. One of the graduate students, when I asked, stated that the enrollment, including the medical school, numbered about 17,000.

As I walked back to my car, parked in the garage between Myers and David Jones, I paused to look at a display window of one of these department stores. There before me was visible evidence of how dependent Australia is on imported goods, and I began thinking of the changes I had observed at home in the past decade. Until about ten years ago it was rare to see foreign goods for sale in the United States other than some very expensive items, the Volkswagen, and the toys manufactured in Hong Kong. Now, however, America is overrun by Toyota, Opel, Sony, Kawasaki, and many other items. But Australia is far ahead of us on this score; foreign goods are extremely common, almost as much as—if not more so than—internally manufactured items. For years the Aussies have sold agricultural products overseas and bought manufactured goods in return. So the Australian is accustomed, even addicted, to foreign goods.

While I was looking in this window, a medium-sized fellow walked up and said, "You're American, aren't you?" I admitted that this was the case, but before I could ask how the man knew this about me he answered, "It's the clothes. I can spot Americans anywhere."

We talked for several minutes, during which time he informed me that he had been a sales representative for a national electronics firm and that before he immigrated to Australia he had been working in Phoenix. "At home I was just existing," he told me, "but here I'm alive. My whole family is alive." People who talk like this always make me want to congratulate them for not being dead, but I did not want to make him angry so I said nothing. Gradually I learned that at present he was working on a sheep run to the north of Adelaide, and that he was trying to learn how to operate his own sheep run, for he hoped to own a place within another year or two. At the age of thirty-four he wanted to hurry to get his own ranch started, but he knew that he could not hurry too much or else he would fail for want of knowledge. "I grew up in a city," he explained, "and I'm trying to learn in five or six years what the eighteen-year-old who grew up on a farm already knows. I'm working here for $250 a month while I'm learning. Of course, we have some savings we brought over from the States: our insurance, which we cashed in; the money from the equity in our house; and what we got when we sold our furniture and our car. We have this in the bank. And thank goodness we came four years ago and didn't lose anything when the United States devalued the dollar."

I asked about his life out on this sheep run. "We don't have a television set out there," he commented, pointing at the sets in the department store window. "Oh, TV reception is available, but we don't want it. It seems like that's all we ever did at home in the evening, watch TV. But without a set now, I never watch."

The more I talked with Americans who had moved to Australia, the more I became convinced that a television set somehow had become a symbol of everything wrong with Americans in the minds of these people. Time and again, they proudly informed me that they do not watch television —implying thereby that their minds were stronger, that they had no more hangnails, and that their breath even smelled better. Just why the television set should become such a symbol is beyond me. Perhaps people intuitively realize that with this thing blaring away, there no longer is so compelling a reason to blabber away at one another.

At last I asked him what he most missed about the States. "I really miss American hotdogs and fried chicken. That's one reason I'm glad to see Kentucky Fried Chicken coming in over here," was his answer. With that I walked away, convinced he had to be something of a madman to eat the stuff, or else was really very lonely for home! In fact, now that I thought about it, I concluded that one reason the Colonel was doing so well in Australia was because of homesick ex-Americans. The same people probably will make McDonald's hamburgers a similar success.

That same evening I noticed in the newspaper a story that roving gangs of thieves and murderers were striking at homes in the Outback. These thugs drop in at some isolated station or another and kill husband, wife, and children, then loot the place at their leisure. According to the story, people living in the Outback were getting suspicious of outsiders, and hospitality was a dying art in remote areas of the country. I thought about my acquaintance of the afternoon working away to learn the sheep-raising trade.

That same newspaper made me aware of just how few differences there were between Australia and home. Just like the governor we elected in Oklahoma in 1970, who pledged never to raise taxes and who then in 1971 soaked us hard, Prime Minister Whitlam and his government, I found, had announced a tentative new tax program designed to soak the rich. That was how our governor at home justified his measure—and a lot of surprised Oklahomans suddenly discovered that according to this formula they were rich. Always when some politician talks about soaking the rich, what happens in the end is that the middle class is going to be hit hard. The rich somehow escape, and the poor have their hand out for something free. So the middle class has to pay. And in Australia there was talk of a tax on capital gains, which would be a dramatic change with past practice in this nation. Also, there was talk of an "Assets Tax," a wild scheme whereby a man's taxes would be based each year not on his income but on his net worth.

The result of this talk was a sudden, dramatic drop in the Australian stock market. In fact, the market here plunged to a low not seen in a decade and more, which caused Dr. Frank Crean, federal treasurer in the Labour government, to declare that share prices were too low; he insisted that the "so-called wisdom men" of the stock market were guilty of "sheer stupidity" in letting prices fall so low.

The following morning we drove down to the ocean (which here is at Gulf St. Vincent) and then north for some distance before returning. Here, as on the road from Melbourne to Adelaide, we noticed the same thing we had seen in Tasmania: there were very, very few billboards in Australia. The roads were not good, neither were they terribly bad. They simply were two-lane strips of bitumen, over which there was not a great deal of traffic and alongside which there were few billboards. I suppose there were few of these means of outdoor advertising because there were so few people on the road to read them.

All too soon noon was approaching, and with it came time to leave Adelaide to catch our train to Perth. I think all of us hated to leave Adelaide, for we had found it a beautiful city.

V.

Out West

ONE OF THE comments we heard most often before we left for Australia was, "You'll find that country much like the United States of some thirty to forty years ago." Well, in the United States of that era, the finest, most elegant way to travel was by passenger train. Flying in those days was something only for the foolhardy (and I suppose to me the only thing that will ever really look like an airplane is one with two wings and an open cockpit; these new things look like darts or rockets, not flying machines). I was very anxious to introduce my children to the experience of riding across the land by rail. My first ride on a train had come in 1950 when at age sixteen I joined the Marine Corps and was sent on the Southern Pacific to San Diego for recruit training.

That ride of twenty-four years before had thrilled me greatly. To those of my generation and older, there was—and still is—something infinitely romantic about trains and the men who ran them. The engineer was a legendary figure to impressionable young lads, more so than the knights of old. His overalls and his denim cap might not have shone like metal, but he was a man in command of an engine that rolled across the land. And that was enough. Even in Australia I could not hope that the engine would be one driven by steam, but for 1974 even the thought of a first-class, transcontinental diesel train ride for my children thrilled me greatly. Therefore, we arrived at the station in Adelaide with more than a few goose bumps on the children—and, if the truth is told, on the adults.

The agent for Commonwealth Railways had told us that the first one hundred miles of our trip, the part from Adelaide to Port Pirie, would be not on the federal railroad but on a train operated by South Australian Railroad (SAR); at Port Pirie we were to transfer to the Trans-Australian. The first part of this trip proved a great disappointment. A porter of uncertain age helped us stow our bags in a chair car, one which had seen far better days, and we set out on time. The countryside reminded me increasingly of New Mexico as we moved north through a flat, level stretch of land given first to agriculture and then increasingly to grazing; in particular I thought of the stretch of road between Clayton and Raton in northeastern New Mexico.

At Port Pirie we disembarked ourselves and our luggage and moved across the station platform to board our reserved compartments on the Trans-Australian. This train, which comes across from Sydney to Broken Hill (a mining town) to Port Pirie, had sleeping cars that were constructed of aluminum and very modern; we were told that these had been manufactured in the United States in 1968 and then were imported into Australia. More important, however, these cars were clean and neat. Richard and Nancy were fascinated by the engineering of our compartments and had to lower their bunks several times to see how these worked.

Our luggage stowed and the bunks back in place, we looked out the windows at Port Pirie. This town of some 17,000 features new schools and bright playground-parks as well as a huge lead smelter. Someone mentioned to us that the city was eager for industry, for the local townsmen wanted progress and prosperity. Therefore, despite heavy unionization, the citizenry would make many concessions to attract employers to their city.

At last the train began to roll, and we sat looking at the scenery first from our compartment and then from the lounge car, which featured upholstered chairs and a piano. Our route was to the north alongside Spencer Gulf to the town of Port Augusta. The countryside really was not very fascinating. It was much like the edge of the Great Plains to the east of the Rockies in Colorado or the high plains country in Montana and Wyoming. A water pipe paralleled the tracks for several miles; it carried drinking water from the Murray River to the city of Port Augusta. It was gradually darkening outside and the land was becoming increasingly barren and flat. We were entering a land where rain rarely falls, but where, of course, they recently had received astonishing amounts of moisture. I could have closed my eyes there, opened them again, and sworn I was in New Mexico. Richard and Nancy, who had never ridden a train (except in amusement parks and short excursion operations), were fascinated with every part of the operation.

Just as darkness fell we were called to dinner. The dining car operated on three shifts. Fortunately we were assigned to the first sitting, and thus we did not have to wait endlessly and watch others go back to be fed while we waited. The meals were efficiently served and very tasty. Inasmuch as we asked for water with our food, our waiter immediately knew us for Americans, and thereafter he gave us particularly good service.

One aspect of Australian life that I have not mentioned and that occurs to me now was the way the locals held their silverware. The true Australian keeps his fork in his left hand at all times, using it *upside down*. He loads the food on the bottom of the fork and transfers it to his mouth rather rapidly. His knife he holds in the palm of his right hand, his index finger extended full length down the back of the blade; with this knife he either cuts portions of meat or else helps load vegetables onto the back of his fork. I tried such an operation but found I lacked expertise at loading food on the bottom of my fork. However, the local people managed nicely.

And there was one young man on the train who, so help me, ate with his knife. I lived the first eight years of my life in the piney woods of East Texas, a region not known for elegant living; but this was the first time I had ever seen someone scooping up food on his knife and thrusting this into his mouth. I must admit the operation worked efficiently—if not aesthetically.

After dinner we returned to the lounge car to play cards. One of the advantages of having just two children, no more and no less, is that it provides a nice foursome. For a time we tried bridge, but the children were still learning it and soon expressed a preference for casino. Eventually, when the third sitting had been fed, the bar opened in the lounge car, the beer that seems to irrigate all of Australia began to flow, people gathered around the piano, and an impromptu "amateur hour" ensued. Australians, I can say from personal experience, sing just as off-key as do Americans under these circumstances. Eventually the tobacco smoke grew too thick, and we retired to our compartments.

The attendant came by to see if we knew how to lower our bunks. Assured that we did, he withdrew, promising to wake us the following morning with a cup of tea. While Richard looked out the window at the scenery, and it could be viewed by the light of a full moon that loaned a ghostly pale mantle to this flat world of few people and little vegetation, I read the newspaper. In this I found that Australia's vaunted arbitration system (whereby no one strikes but rather lets a federal agency arbitrate the wage dispute) was breaking down. According to the paper the unionists were "disenchanted" with the wage increases they had been receiving during this time of inflation. Truck drivers were demanding more money and talking of going on strike (we had just left a United States where the truckers had tried to organize a nationwide strike). And this talk of strikes in Australia was at a time when the Labour party was in power.

At last we turned off the lights in the compartment which Richard and I shared, and we talked as we looked out on the moonlit landscape. Our bunks were long and comfortable, and there was little swaying, just the steady clackety-clack of the wheels going down the rails.

We were awakened by a knock on the door the next morning, and there was our attendant with a cup of hot tea for each of us. Looking outside, we found ourselves halted at a tiny station. I immediately dressed and walked outside, stepping down to get my feet on solid ground. I could look away to the horizon, and in every direction the land was so flat that I seemed to be looking up at the horizon. This was the Nullarbor (literally "nil trees") Plain; it was as flat as all the pictures showed it, and there were indeed no trees.

When the train began to move again, I noted ponds of water standing here and there. The attendant told me that the weather had been unusual this year, for the rains had been heavy indeed. Despite the lateness of the autumn, the grass was green and apparently covered the earth to a depth of ten inches to a foot. It, along with shrubs such as myall, mulga, and malee (short, alien-looking plants about a foot or so high), was moving with a wavelike motion because of the winds that were blowing. The attendant also informed us to be on the lookout for dingoes, kangaroos, and even foxes.

After breakfast, which proved to be yet another good meal, we sat in the lounge car and looked at the scenery. There is little in the United States to which I might compare the Nullarbor. For some eight hundred kilometers there was virtually nothing higher than one foot. At the western end of the plain, near Kalgoorlie, we began to see scrub oak (they call it bull oak) and sheep. But on the plain itself, there was little to look at. In fact, at one point on the Nullarbor there was the "long straight," a stretch of track that for 478 kilometers (297 miles) had no turns or curves whatsoever. This, we were told, was the longest straight stretch of track anywhere in the world.

Small communities of railroad workers were spaced about thirty-five kilometers apart along the right of way. Every one of these towns looked alike, for they consisted of a dozen or so identical homes and a depot. About the only difference in these little clusters was the type of abandoned automobiles rusting away at the edge of them. The desperation of the people along the track was evident at Cook, a refueling point for the diesel locomotives and thus, with two hundred people, much larger than most of these towns. In front of the hospital in this town was a sign stating, "Hospital needs your help. Please get sick." At all the other little towns there was a landing strip with a windsock; this, we were told, was for the famed flying doctor service. And each village had a stock of drugs, each bearing a number; when someone got ill, he could call on the radio, talk to the doctor, and be told the number of the drug he should take. Serious cases were flown out to a major hospital.

The Nullarbor is a place that the ocean once covered, and thus it really is just a vast limestone plain. This limestone, which came from crustacean shells of millions of years ago, is covered by red dirt apparently about an inch or two thick. Water, when it does fall in the form of rain, is rapidly absorbed into this porous plain. But so much had fallen this year that it seemed to be standing everywhere.

As I looked at the people on this train, our fellow passengers, I became aware that nationalities are set apart more than just by the external things such as haircuts and styles of clothing. Little things, which usually do not occur to us, give away our nationality: our mannerisms, our facial expressions, our hand gestures, our posture, our way of walking, and our way of just looking at one another. Together all of these minor things join to shout, "I am an American," or, "I am an Australian" or some other "ian." We are not aware of these mannerisms in ourselves or even in those around us who are of the same nationality. Thus when in some strange land we notice these at the subconscious level, they tell us in an uneasy sort of way that we are among foreigners or in a comforting way that we are among like-minded fellows. Even our ordinary expressions do the same thing. For some slight fault the American will say, "Pardon me, " or, "Excuse me," while the Australian almost always says, "Sorry." For our "good" or "okay," they say "beaut" (short for *beautiful*). It is very easy to find yourself imitating these things quickly in order to try to blend in (and we all hate to be conspicuous) or else as an aid to communication. And the more we imitate the things that at first seem foreign, the sooner we are made to feel among people who are not strangers.

Eventually the long straight gave way to gentle curves, shrubs could be seen, then stunted trees, and finally sheep grazing away to make wool and lamb chops. At last in the distance we saw two kangaroos jumping along, a sight that caused great excitement among the passengers who crowded to one side and looked. For a time the two seemed to be keeping abreast of the train, but at last they fell back. We then could return to our card game—and most of the Australians to their drinking. We never did see any dingoes or foxes.

Just at dark we arrived at the town of Kalgoorlie, a place where Herbert Hoover as a young man directed mining activities. Now it was a city of 23,000, and building lots here were cheap. According to the evening newspaper, housing could be had most reasonably: $5,950 for a two-bedroom brick house; another two-bedroom, plaster-lined house was for sale for $3,500 with only $700 down; still another home, advertised as weatherboard, plaster-lined, and with an attractive garden, was up for $7,500. This same newspaper stated that the price of bread was up three cents a loaf in Victoria, and that in Perth the drivers of milk trucks were on strike, bringing a forecast of a rise in milk prices in the near future. Also, the paper noted, litter was as much a problem here as in the States, for antilitter drives were being conducted. This same newspaper, as well as others we had read, reflected a great fear of drug use by youngsters. An American in Melbourne had told me, "I came to Australia to escape drugs in the high schools and even the junior high schools back home. Now it is here, and I don't know where I can move next."

Just as I finished reading all this cheerful news, someone gave me a newspaper from Adelaide. In it I saw where K. W. Lewis, head of Engineering and Water Service for that city, had stated that the public water supply for Adelaide would not meet the standards of the World Health Organization. We had noted that the water there was murky brown and tasted heavily of chlorine. Mr. Lewis did state that work was going forward to remedy the defects. I said nothing to Laura about this; she was just recovering from the shot she had received in Fiji, and I did not want her worrying about this.

And this newspaper carried a story about a movement in South Australia to speed up the introduction of equal pay for equal work by women. I reflected on all the problems listed in these two papers: inflation, strikes, drugs, women's rights, and unhealthy water—and began to wonder what Americans might come to Australia to escape. All the same problems seemed to be here.

On this trip we had met two couples from America, both of them immigrants. When I asked the first couple why they had moved to Australia, the man answered, "At home I was a liberal Democrat and a member of the Sierra Club. We gave about $500 a year to various liberal causes, and at election time we worked for the election of the candidate we hoped would change America. But we grew tired when we couldn't see any real progress! We had worked hard within the system, but nothing changed no matter who was elected at the local, state, and national levels. So we decided to quit and leave."

I asked them about the "causes" they supported in Australia and if Australia was moving in some directions that America might imitate. "No, I don't guess so," he shrugged. "Actually I haven't checked on movements and causes here. We're just living our own life."

The other couple echoed the same sentiment. Said the man, "I gave up on the United States when the people there failed to elect George McGovern president. I decided then and there, 'The hell with it.' And we left." I asked about his political affiliations in Australia and was he active. "No," he replied, "I'm not." At least he had the decency to look sheepish about his noninvolvement now.

"What," I wanted to know, "is most attractive about Australia?"

"Life here is less competitive," the first fellow said. "I go home for lunch almost every day, and our children seem closer here. They take piano lessons, go horseback riding, swim. And it doesn't cost as much."

His wife chipped in, "We save enough on their clothes to pay for most of their lessons. The stores here don't carry such a big selection of children's clothing because they all wear uniforms to school. And all the mothers seem to sew more. I've learned to sew, and we save a lot of money not buying them many things to wear."

"People here do a lot of exchanging and swapping," commented the second man. "We spent our last vacation here at a cottage on the beach, one which was loaned to us by friends and thus which was free. I go fishing at the beach or at a public lake now, and this costs almost nothing. Back in the States, on a weekend when I wanted to fish, I had to go to a private lake, stay at some resort, and spend a hundred dollars. But here, for almost no cost at all, I seem to catch about as many fish. Perhaps even more fish, for here I don't drink as much and so I spend more time fishing."

And his wife echoed the same thoughts as those of the first couple: "Here we borrow more, share more, swap more. There's more neighborliness. I like it."

This conversation seemed to reinforce what I had heard in Melbourne and in Adelaide. What all of them seemed to be trying to say was, "Here we aren't in the rat race." But what they were escaping that they believed bad in America was big-city life, *not* the United States as a whole! At any time these people had wanted to do so, they could have changed their lifestyle to something less competitive, and without moving. However, it apparently was easier to change your lifestyle at some moment of dramatic shift, such as a move to Australia, than it was when you remained in the same town and at the same job.

At the end of the conversation with these Americans, I asked about the economics of living in Australia. Again came the same refrain about the "rat race," but in a different way. One of the men told me, "Even making less money here, I still enjoy a lifestyle better than I had at home. I live fifteen miles north of Perth in one of the suburbs on the beach. There are miles of beach to the north that are deserted. I can swim and fish and not be bothered by people. And I pay only sixty dollars a month at the country club, which is only a ten-minute drive from our home. When I get out there, I rarely have to wait more than twenty or thirty minutes to get out on the first hole."

I bit my tongue and did not tell him that in Stillwater my dues at the country club were only fifty dollars a month (American money) and that I could golf almost any time I wanted without waiting more than ten minutes. This fellow's problem, as with most Americans I met in Australia, seemed to be that he believed the disadvantages of city life were universal in America. He could have found a better America by moving to a smaller town rather than all the way to Australia.

At 8:00 A.M. we arrived at the downtown railroad station in Perth, checked out our automobile from Avis—a red Ford Falcon—and drove downtown. This car proved to be the best we drove in Australia. In Perth we found a new high-rise Sheraton Hotel overlooking the Swan River. In the coffeeshop downstairs we drank the first decent coffee we had tasted in this country. Then, upstairs, we showered, changed clothes, and prepared to explore the city of Perth.

Looking back on the past two days of riding on the train, something dawned on me. Richard had loved the train ride, and Nancy had loved it for about a day before getting bored. Our compartments ("cabins," the Australians call them) had been comfortable, containing closets, a toilet, a basin, and a shower, but all had been cramped and not conducive to comfortable living. But riding an airplane for three hours is infinitely easier and more comfortable than any train ever invented. Passenger trains died in America for a very good reason! And those of us who look back with longing and regret to the passing of the railroad are fooling ourselves. No, the good old days were not thirty or forty years ago. They are right now. We decided to sell the other half of our roundtrip tickets and fly back across the continent.

Laura went downstairs to the beautyshop in the basement of the Sheraton to get her hair washed and set. While there she fell into conversation with a young girl from Philadelphia. This young girl explained that her family loved to travel, did so extensively. Laura asked if the young girl had ever been in Oklahoma only to receive a snort in reply.

Suddenly this young girl began explaining her whole life and all her problems to Laura. It seemed that she was in Perth to get as far away from her parents as possible, that she loved it in Perth, but that she was making only eighty-five dollars a week at her work (which she never identified), and that this was not enough for her to live on. Next she tried to beg a cigarette from Laura, who does not smoke. Failing there, the girl asked one of the attendants in the beautyshop for a cigarette—this while she was getting a tint and permanent. The attendants laughed at her, one of them saying that for fifty cents she would get the girl a package of her own.

This young lady proved to have a real store of hatred for the United States. Soon she was railing against then-President Nixon, saying he should be impeached. However, she could give no good reason for this except to say that he was embarrassing the United States. Little did she apparently realize how much she personally was accomplishing the same end. I suspected, from listening to Laura tell about this encounter, that the young lady from Philadelphia came to the Sheraton to meet Americans because she was homesick. However, in the process she was putting on airs that hurt her efforts, as do many people in her category. For example, her extensive travels, from what Laura could learn, consisted, prior to her trip to Australia, of one journey to Florida.

Laura soon ended the conversation by quietly defending the United States, and the workers in the beautyshop apparently loved it. They began laughing at Miss Philadelphia when Laura pushed her to defend her anti-American opinions with facts, and the shopworkers ended by telling the girl to buy her own cigarettes. I guess ugly Americans abroad probably begin as ugly Americans at home.

While we were in the Sheraton, I met several Americans connected with the mining industry. To the northeast of Perth, on the northwest coast of Australia, huge deposits of iron ore had been found, along with some oil. These people were quite in contrast to Miss Philadelphia. They had come to Australia because of the opportunity to make money and for the adventure, not to escape something. They talk positively about the United States and, from what I could tell, create a good impression for the country. Yet these people have succeeded so well that they have raised some anti-Yankee feelings about the amount of American ownership of local corporations. As one American businessman told me, "These people don't want to put up any risk capital for new exploration, as, for example, in oil. However, the minute we bring in some wells and develop a producing field, then the Aussies want in. And if we don't let them in, then they begin complaining about American ownership and start talking about getting some new legislation passed requiring a certain percentage of local ownership. So we let them in."

I think some of this local feeling against Americans—which sounds suspiciously like Canadian feelings—stemmed from

World War II, when American servicemen were here and wooed Australian girls. The American servicemen were rich compared with Australians. And many of the Australian men were off fighting in Europe.

I guess there always is hatred of a foreign nationality that is better off economically than the locals.

That afternoon we went to the horse races at Belmont Park. In the seventh race a horse named Pecos Bill was running, and we made a hunch bet that he would win. Alas, the hunch failed. Pecos Bill did not live up to the qualities of his namesake; he finished fourth. Thank goodness my hunch was not that strong, for I ventured a whole fifty cents on him. Here they do have a fifty-cent window along with a one-dollar window, something strange to us, for we had been conditioned to the two-dollar bet as the smallest available.

The Australian horse players seemed not as demonstrative as American bettors at the track. These people bet with far more concentration and dedication than ever I had seen. And they took their time doing it, for the races ran forty-five minutes apart, not twenty or twenty-five as at home. I did not get the impression that the fans enjoyed the racing as much as Americans; instead, they seemed, in European fashion, to be trying to strike it rich, and thus the entire affair was very serious.

When we returned to the hotel, I began to feel the onset of some sickness. I guessed it was my turn, for Laura was feeling much better. Inasmuch as flu had been sweeping Sydney when we were there—and, according to the papers, the Sydney flu epidemic was widespread—I knew what I had.

Richard and Nancy, in exploring everything in our room, pointed out that the Sheraton Perth was the first hotel in which we had stayed that there were no facilities for making tea. All the others had provided an electric pot for heating water along with cups, saucers, tea bags, instant coffee, powdered milk, and sugar. Inasmuch as the rooms were twenty-four dollars each (that would be thirty-six dollars

American), I guess it was appropriate that they did not have these facilities; always the most expensive place seemed to provide the least in the way of service.

The following morning I was running a slight fever, so I swallowed some aspirin along with half a quart of orange juice, and then I propped myself up in bed to read the newspaper while Laura and the children shopped. In the letters-to-the-editor column I found a long complaint about how inept repairmen at garages were robbing the public; the writer wanted some type of competency test administered to mechanics by the state. California has been doing just this for the past year, but in Oklahoma I have for years been paying too much for poor work.

Another writer to the editor was complaining about the "scaling test" that was used to judge the matriculation of students from the public schools. This test is important because it determines who can go to college and the university. The writer was incensed because the test used a high percentage of questions related to Australian and Anglo-Saxon culture, something he claimed was unfair to the New Australians (immigrants since World War II, many of whom have been from Southern and Eastern Europe). This is another of those issues that crop up in other parts of the world. It made me think in particular about the complaints of black Americans that test questions are white-oriented. Yet I could not help wondering where the writer of this letter thought he was living; obviously he was living in Australia, and the questions there obviously should relate to Australia, a country with an Anglo-Saxon culture. The liberals apparently were the same here as at home: ashamed of their own culture and trying to be one-worlders.

The next day, Sunday, we did little but rest. We did go to church, St. Andrews Presbyterian, in the morning. I think churches must smell the same everywhere: a blend of furniture polish and candle wax. The women in the church all had on hats, and many of them also wore gloves; it had been years since American women in church all came in hat and gloves. Moreover, almost all the members were elderly; I thought this very strange until I remembered that this was a downtown church. To my great surprise the minister, to whom we were introduced at the church door just as we entered, was wearing a Roman collar. And inside the flag was English, not Australian. The sermon—well, sermons are the same the world over.

On television that afternoon, as I nursed the last of my flu, there was an interview with a fellow living near Alice Springs. An immigrant from Vienna, he was training camels with the intention of using them to give tours of the Outback. He intended eventually to have twelve of the beasts and use them for his tourist operation. Apparently he liked camels, for he kept referring to them as "marvelous beasts." I guess there is no animal so unlovely but what someone falls in love with it.

The next morning we drove to Fremantle, the port city for Perth, and then went on down the coast to Mandurah. On the way we stopped at Madora Beach to allow the children to splash in the Indian Ocean. Laura was standing near the water trying to get a picture of the children when a big wave rolled up and filled her shoes—dampening her enthusiasm somewhat. Later we drove past Mandurah to a place called Miami Beach because Nancy wanted to take some pictures and had forgotten to take them earlier.

On our drive back toward Perth, which took us inland near the Darling Range of mountains, I again was impressed by the trees. Of all the sights I would see in Australia, I think the one that will remain with me longest is the trees—twisted and gnarled and ghostly white, looking a million years old. They seemed more suitable to the moon or to some other planet than to this world. These are gum trees, mostly eucalyptus.

That evening we went out to dinner, and again I noticed that no one drank water or milk. Nowhere in the country did we find public water fountains, nor did they bring it at restaurants. On the table when you arrived were tea cups (as with coffee cups at home); apparently that was all Australians drank, that and alcoholic beverages. As at Adelaide, there was a local wine about which everyone bragged; we tried it and found it good, but nothing to write home to grandmother about. And Swan Beer, the local brew, was excellent. The brewery sat beside the Swan River, and at night the lights on it could be seen from most parts of town. One interesting thing about Perth: here they did serve the beer cold, whereas in other parts of Australia it was served a little below room temperature, as in England.

And how they smoked! I think I inhaled more nicotine here just by breathing than I did at home smoking my pipe. Every other commercial on television seemed to be the Marlboro man—or was I just more conscious of this, having been off cigarettes about a month?

On the subject of restaurants, I have changed my mind about the need for a chain of medium-priced eating establishments. For a time I thought such a chain would do quite well, but by the time we had been in Perth a few days I knew better. The men seemed to eat out only in order to drink, and the women ate out principally at noon while shopping. In order to sell drinks the restaurateur must have a first-class license and run a first-class establishment, and thus a chain of good but moderately priced restaurants would get no business in the evenings.

Strolling down St. George's Terrace, a main street in downtown Perth (a street that suddenly becomes Adelaide Terrace in the maddening way that streets in Mexico City suddenly change names), you see one of the loveliest cities on any continent suddenly taking shape. Government House, wherein the federal offices are housed, is a modern structure of concrete and glass, as are the office buildings of downtown. But the talk in this city is not leisurely; it is that of a New York City in the making: of oil refineries and steelworks just twenty miles to the south at Kwinana; of the iron ore to the north being shipped to Japan; of discoveries of bauxite, nickel, and natural gas in the state; of the big dam on the Ord River that is opening vast amounts of agricultural lands for the growing of cotton and grain; and even of lobster and shrimp fisheries where the output is flown by air express to the West Coast of the United States. All around Perth are handsome suburbs, which contrast with the twenty- and thirty-story skyscrapers of downtown.

We decided that we would take a small vacation from our hectic traveling, and for the next four days we relaxed by driving to Bunbury, some one hundred ten miles to the south. This brought us through small resorts that seemed like the villages along the coast of Maine or in New Hampshire. We heard of the giant Karri trees, which, we were told, are larger than the redwoods of California, but we did not visit that region. Nor did we go on around the southwestern tip of Australia to visit the town of Albany or further east to Esperance. It is at this last-named town that American entertainer Art Linkletter has huge property holdings of grazing land. The area around Esperance, one fellow told me, is scrub desert land that has been made productive through the efforts of research scientists in Canberra. These scientists discovered that certain trace elements were missing, and they showed that by mixing these with the fertilizer, the region would grow good grass to fatten sheep (and attract kangaroos to compete with the sheep).

During this time at Bunbury I met an American immigrant working in a garage whose comments gave me additional insight into Australia. This forty-year-old former resident of Salt Lake City said, "At home I had to work like hell to make enough to put my kids through school. Of course, all their friends in junior high and high school were talking about going on to college. But I noticed that when my friends' kids got through college, they looked on their parents like dirt. Here in Australia you don't have to worry so much about putting up money for college because that's all taken care of by the government. And medical care here is good, and the costs are very low."

I asked about the government's policies in the area of child care. He replied, "I got an allowance for them when they were young. Now that they're about to finish the public schools, I know that they can go to the university on scholarship if they pass all the necessary tests. Otherwise they can go to work like I had to, and nobody here'll think any less of them just because they work with their hands."

When I asked about the government's social programs that would help him, he likewise was happy: "I know here that when I'm old I'll get a good pension. Oh, when my kids are grown and on their own, I know the government's gonna take about half of what I make, but I don't care. We get our money's worth here."

This attitude contrasted sharply with what another American had told me in Perth. A farmer in the Ord River area, this fellow had informed me: "Australia is no place to get rich if you're a blue-collar worker, but it does offer real good possibilities if you're a farmer. I think this is the best place on earth for farming."

The mechanic in Bunbury did have some complaints about his new home, however. "Life is changing here," he told me. "When I first came over six years ago, people didn't seem to care so much about what kind of car you drove or how new your refrigerator or how big your television set was. But now it is beginning to matter. Life is getting more competitive, just like at home, and people are more conscious of the things you own. Every now and then I start to get disgusted with the way things are going here, and I think about going back to the States. But then I think, 'If it's like that here, just imagine what it's like now back in the States.' And so I stay on."

I asked him about the friendships he had been able to form in Western Australia, and he grew warm about the country again: "Australians don't make friends as fast," he said. "They're not so given to backslapping as Americans. But once you're accepted as one of them—as a mate—friendships are stronger than they were at home. Here they'll loan you their car or their house or even money faster than the so-called friends I had back home."

Late on Saturday we drove back to Perth and checked in at a motel. On this drive we took Highway 1 which runs about fifteen miles in from the ocean. Actually Highway 1 is the pride of Australia. It begins in northern Queensland and runs all the way around the continent, south to Brisbane and Sydney, across to Melbourne, west to Adelaide, across the Nullarbor to Perth, and on around the northwest to Darwin. The last few hundred miles from Darwin around to northern Queensland have not been completed—and may never be, for that region is still a very raw and rough territory where wandering aborigines are known to kill white interlopers. Highway 1 stretches for 20,000 miles. But I can say from personal experience that it is not a freeway. Far from it, for it is almost all two-lane road about the same in appearance as our national roads of two or three decades ago.

Back in Perth on Sunday morning we again attended St. Andrews Presbyterian Church. This time one of the deacons, who owned a hardware store locally, told us about his two trips to the United States and offered his opinions. His first trip, he said, had taken him to New York City and Las Vegas, while his second journey had allowed him to visit in Illinois and Kentucky. His view was that he had seen less litter in the United States than in Australia and that he had vastly liked his trips. He also spoke of an American resident in Perth for forty years who had postured himself to one and all as an authority on things American, but who, the deacon had learned, was years out of date about conditions in the United States.

This deacon was correct in his comment about litter. In Perth we noted that the sidewalks were filled with litter. Almost every adult smoked, and all apparently loved to throw their cigarette butts on the sidewalk. Paper was blowing here and there everywhere we went.

Contrasting with the litter of downtown was the beauty of King's Park, which we visited that afternoon. An area almost equal in size to the downtown section of Perth, it has been set aside for gardens. But just a decade or so ago it was expanded. Sitting there on a hill overlooking the town and Swan River, the park has twenty-five acres of botanic gardens in which you can see examples of every species of West Australian plants. The names have a magical ring to them: sheoaks, tuarts, marri, jarrah, kangaroo paws, spider orchids, boronia, and everlastings. Here we did see a few of the giant Karri trees, but they as yet were not sufficiently large to drown out our memory of California's redwoods. Western Australia is famed for its wildflowers, which, according to what we were told, bloom in the spring and carpet the desert with beauty. Unfortunately we were there during the winter and did not get to see this carpet of beauty. However, King's Park did give us some clue as to the loveliness of the state.

And King's Park gives a clue to the loveliness of other areas, for six acres in it have been set aside for plants from South Africa, the Mediterranean, and even from California. The stimulus for the development and expansion of King's Park came from conservationists concerned that the incoming industries and graziers would kill off much of the desert, and that people would forget what these plants looked like. In fact, at King's Park the botanists were trying to preserve some of the types of wildflowers that otherwise might have disappeared. How I wish many of the conservationists at home would direct their energies into something so concrete and beneficial as the equivalent of King's Park instead of running off at the mouth about things abstract. Those who want to protest litter should pick up beer cans; those concerned with damage to the environment should help found something like King's Park.

The following morning, our last full day in Perth, I went out to visit the University of Western Australia while Laura and the children shopped for souvenirs. To get there I had to drive along the banks of the Swan River alongside King's Park three or four miles to the town of Crawley, a suburb marked by beautiful homes and lovely yards. The university advertises that its architecture is modern, but tempered by a Renaissance style. However, to me it looked like modified Spanish Renaissance (very similar to the buildings of some of the Spanish missions of Southern California); the bricks are a warm yellowish brown and the roofs of red tile. There on a lovely river setting, the campus takes pride in its replica of an Elizabethan theater where the plays of Shakespeare are performed by aspiring actors and actresses.

For years I had been interested in similarities in ranching, farming, and mining in the American West and the Australian Outback, and I spent the day poring over sources in the library of this great institution. At lunch I wandered across the campus and, as in Adelaide, felt immediately as though I were in the United States on some major university campus. There seems little difference between their universities and ours, even as to the democratic air about them; their schools, like those in the United States, are more open to poor youngsters of merit than those of Europe—although I am certain that having money does open more doors than merit.

Reading the newspaper that evening I noted that housing in Perth apparently was most reasonable, the most I had seen anywhere in Australia except Kalgoorlie. A new home of eleven squares (which is how they advertise the size of houses; a square is one hundred square feet) could be had for $10,348, according to one ad; this was a house of three bedrooms and one bath. On the subject of housing, we had noticed in driving around Perth that the tile on the roofs of houses here was of white, blue, black, and even green, along with the orange (or red) tile, which we had seen everywhere else in Australia.

The next morning we went to the airport to catch a plane for Sydney. In purchasing our tickets I reflected that no money except American seems like real currency. The Australian money, which comes in denominations of $1, $2, $5, $10, $20, and $50—and each of which is a different size (the one-dollar bill is smallest and then each denomination gets progressively larger)—seems like play money. However, my attitude toward it was made more realistic by remembering how much it cost; $100.00 American brought $66.61 (minus six cents for a stamp tax). I guess only the money that you normally handle seems like genuine currency.

At the airport newsstand I was visibly reminded of just how openly available is pornography in Australia. Books with nude females on the covers were out where they could easily be seen by children.

As we waited to board the plane I read the morning Perth newspaper and noted that free polio immunization clinics were being advertised in the city. And I saw where Prime Minister Whitlam had just announced that the federal budget for the following year would be one of "austerity," designed to hold inflation to an annual rate of ten percent. One columnist commented that while the prime minister and his cohorts were talking about the federal budget, "the rest of us are back to worrying about the higher taxes we expect."

However, most of the space in the Perth newspaper was taken up with arguments about allowing stores to remain open in the evenings. We had noted that almost everything in the city (as in other Australian cities) shut down entirely on Saturday afternoon and Sunday, but this fuss was about allowing the stores to stay open on weekday evenings. In Western Australia the state law and the "Shop Assistants' Union" (that means clerks) forbade stores to remain open in the evenings. In fact, store hours were set both by law and by union rules at 8:00 A.M. to 6:00 P.M. five days a week and 8:00 A.M. to 1:00 P.M. on Saturday. The government of Western Australia was discussing the passage of a law that would follow the example of New South Wales (Sydney) and that would allow stores to remain open late one night a week; the proposed law stipulated that employees working that night would get time off during the day to compensate for this rather than give "penalty rates" (overtime pay). However, the clerks' union was adamantly opposed to the proposed law.

The newspaper, in discussing the situation, noted that stores in resort areas of New South Wales and Queensland were allowed to have unrestricted hours for fifteen weeks of the year. This allowed these stores to stay open as long as they wished during the tourist season (spring school holidays, Christmas, and autumn school holidays). And stores in Sydney were allowed to stay open one night a week during the rest of the year, allowing everyone to shop with his family; even the clerks could work late only every other week, allowing them to shop with their families at least every two weeks.

Finally this paper noted that the Perth symphony, which was to open shortly under the baton of a guest European conductor, was to be opened with the playing of a didgeridoo. In fact, an aborigine was to play this six-foot-long primitive instrument. This was being done, I read, to give the occasion a true Australian flavor. My thought was, as the airplane departed, that few Australians probably had ever heard one of those things; moreover, it did not truly represent the culture of the land. I guess the Australians, like Americans, will soon be wallowing in a sea of national guilt about the plight of their aborigines and trying to atone for the sins of the past. There even had been a token aborigine—from the mission—at the worship services at St. Andrews Presbyterian Church the last Sunday we were there. I guess people everywhere need to feel guilty about something.

Looking back at the vast state we were leaving, we concluded that Western Australia had in many ways reminded us of Texas, for it is huge and there is in the state a strong feeling of separate identity. The people there still talk periodically about separating from the rest of Australia and forming their own nation, while signs within the state encourage "buying Western Australia."

And we found this a state filled with Americans. Some had come because in the far Outback they could carry a gun and feel at one with Tom Mix and Gene Autry. For this type the "Old West" lives again—with an Australian accent. Even the towns to the east and north of Perth apparently encourage this kind of feeling, for they closely resemble the boom towns of the West. Movies supposedly taking place in Nevada or Arizona could be shot here, and few people would be the wiser.

Yet other Americans come for the business or agricultural opportunities. One former Yankee told us in Perth that he had come Down Under because he had been recruited much like the Army seeks enlistees. An Australian team had visited his hometown in West Texas to show a film pointing out the opportunities for getting rich in the Ord River area. This fellow said he had come—and that he was glad, for here he was making a twenty-five percent return on his investment every year. He also commented that so many of his neighbors were American that he felt right at home, and that his children, despite living in Australia, were growing up just the way he wanted them to: "Like I did. For them it's like growing up before cities got so big in America. I'm real happy for them—and for the money I'm making in Western Australia."

VI.

Sydney, Canberra, and the Outback

OUR FLIGHT EASTWARD was to go from Perth to Melbourne and then on to Sydney. Inasmuch as it departed about 11:15 A.M. for the two and one-half-hour flight to Melbourne, we became hungry after about an hour and a half of flying, for the tea and biscuit served us were not sufficient for the day's needs. At last I stopped one of the stewardesses and asked when we might expect to eat. It was then that we learned a hard lesson about flying in Australia: the domestic airlines here do not feed those passengers flying economy class. Only first-class passengers in Australia are presumed to get hungry, this in a country where democracy supposedly reigns supreme. During the forty-minute layover in Melbourne, we dashed into the airport, assured a minion of the government that we were carrying no fruit, and then bolted something down at the quick food counter.

During that flight we talked extensively with this stewardess, who proved articulate and insightful. She told us that most of the Americans she had met in Australia had moved there from Los Angeles, San Francisco, Chicago, or New York City, and that their stated reasons for moving were to escape violence, crime, and the drug problem. However, said she, these same Americans, when they arrived in Australia, tended to settle in Sydney or Melbourne—which are just as crime-ridden, have just as much violence, and have problems with readily available drugs.

Next she asked about the extent of our travels in Australia, whereupon we explained where we had been and where we yet hoped to go. And in answer to her question, we told her that we were not on any package tour. "That's good," she said, "for no one has as bad an image in Australia as American tourists." I asked why. "Because of the groups of little ladies who come over on a package tour," she replied. "They come over, spending their deceased husbands' insurance money and making all kinds of demands in their hotels and on the airplanes. But they don't really see anything or understand anything. They might just as well be in Afghanistan as Australia," she snorted.

After serving tea to Laura and me and Coca-Cola to the children (the Coke naturally bottled in Perth), she continued the conversation by asking about the appliances in Laura's kitchen. "After going almost all over the world," she said, "I've come to the conclusion that American women have it better than anyone else." When we asked her why she had come to this decision, she replied, "All those appliances." It soon became apparent that a dishwashing machine is *the* status symbol for Australian women. "And some young American stewardesses from Pan Am with whom I roomed," this stewardess wailed, "couldn't understand why our apartment didn't have a built-in dishwasher, to say nothing of a washer and dryer furnished in each apartment."

When we questioned her about the price of apartments and housing, she told us that she and her husband currently were moving from Sydney to Melbourne and pricing housing in Victoria's capital city. She told us that the normal-sized lot in both cities is 60' x 120' and cost between $15,000 and

$25,000 depending on location. Houses in Australia normally are sold separate from the lot; you look at a model of the house you want and are told it will cost a set amount provided your lot is level (and what we call a "lot," they refer to as a "block"). You buy your block and then you order your house, and this is extremely expensive.

Running throughout this stewardess's talk was a lament about inflation. "Last year," she wailed, "I paid $1.30 for a whole leg of lamb. Now that same leg of lamb costs $2.70."

One of the questions I asked was about the large number of travel agencies we had seen in Australia. I raised this point to elicit some response about the Aussies' attitude toward travel. "All of them expect four weeks of paid vacation every year," she replied, "and they want to take it somewhere other than at home." She went on to explain that normally in Australia a worker can expect three weeks of vacation for the first four or five years he is with a company, four weeks of vacation for the next five or so years, and after twelve years he gets a three-month leave with pay.

"Yes," she went on, "Aussies do love their vacation. In fact, few of them like to work at all and seem to live for their time off." It was for this reason, she explained, that almost all shop stewards in the unions are British immigrants. Australians do not want this job, which, although it requires little work, demands long hours. "Aussies," she said, "want to work their thirty-five or forty hours a week and go to a pub. The New Australians, the Greek or Italian immigrants, are working double and even triple shifts to make money and acquire all the things they want. So that leaves the British to be shop stewards. They don't mind the long hours as long as they don't have to work. About ninety percent of all shop stewards in Australia are British," she concluded.

As to where Australians travel on their vacations, she noted that the package tour with prepaid ground arrangements was very popular. Singapore and Fiji seemed to be the places to go. "When I first flew into Singapore for Qantas," she said, "the ugly whites were the Americans.

Now it is the Australians. Many Aussies are quite shocked to discover that the local people there hate us badly and see us as big, drunken, overspending, loafing Caucasians."

Arriving in Sydney at last, we found it astonishingly cold. When I commented about this to the fellow at the Avis Rent-a-Car counter, he replied that a "southerly" had just blown in. Apparently this is the antipodal equivalent of our Oklahoma "northers," which bring the cold down from the North Pole. Here it comes from the South Pole, with nothing in between, not even the proverbial "barbed-wire fence," which we talk about at home as the only thing standing between us and that shoddy Canadian cold weather.

We checked out a Ford Tourina, a British Ford designed by some sadist to scrape knuckles and bruise knees, and checked into one of the Flag Inns. The prices for supper proved to be the highest we had encountered in Australia, something we would find almost uniformly in Sydney, a city that likes to think of itself as first in Australia in every way.

That night on television we were treated to yet more old American series. All the capital cities so far (and we had watched in Melbourne, Hobart, Adelaide, and Perth) have Channel 2; this is the Australian Broadcasting Corporation (or ABC). Most of these cities also have channels 7 and 9, along with a couple that had Channel 10; these three are straight commercial channels, two of which seem to be "networks," in a loose sense of the word. The staple on all of these is old American series. Even ABC runs such series as "Sesame Street," "Lassie," "Andy Pandy," "Cisco Kid," "Superman," and cartoons and movies; it also serves up "This Week in Britain" and several British series, some of which are astonishingly outspoken and frank (that is, they make rather explicit references to sex). However, the channels do offer a rough rating system for their shows. For example, when "All in the Family" runs (and it does show there), an announcer tells viewers that the show is not suitable for children.

Also, I noted in the evening paper that Al Grassby, the defeated member of Parliament who served as minister for immigration and who was defeated in the last election (but who could serve for three months after losing), told an audience here last night that Australia could not get away with erecting a "Kangaroo Curtain around itself to keep out blacks and yellows." Apparently the gentleman did not yet understand what democracy was all about. In a democracy an elected official is supposed to *represent* the views of his constituents—and Grassby's constituents turned him out of office for representing a racial view different from their own. But at least the voters turned him out of office. At home many congressmen and legislators do not represent their constituents' views, and they keep getting reelected.

The following day we decided the best way to begin any tour of Sydney would be to look from atop the AMP building, which is fifty stories tall, the highest in Australia. Once atop this structure the visitor forgets the small fee charged for going up to the viewing platform, for the view is great. Sydney spreads out before you: a modern city of skyscrapers housing banks and insurance companies, a government office building twenty-five stories high, a new Hilton Hotel. All these crowd right down toward the shore of Sydney's harbor—and the Opera House. I really do believe nothing else can be said of this structure that has not been said already, and four or five times each. It is breathtaking in conception, sweeping in execution, a glimpse of the spirit of the land. At least that is what the manufacturers of aluminum siding for homes advertise, saying that the cost of this structure would have been much cheaper but just as permanent if only it had been made with aluminum siding. Such is the prominence of this structure that almost everyone wants to use it in advertising for everything from headstones to hernia aids.

Meanwhile, across the way we could see the Harbour (I must remember to use the *u* in spelling that) Bridge. This bridge was for many years what the Opera House has become overnight—the symbol of Sydney, even of Australia. A single arch linking downtown Sydney with its northern suburbs, the Harbour Bridge is 170 feet above the sea and 1,650 feet between its arches. People in Sydney are as proud of their bridge as the residents of San Francisco are of the Golden Gate.

The roof line of the Opera House looks like the sails of a ship, while the Harbour Bridge is sufficiently high to allow any ship afloat to pass under it. It is appropriate that both these symbols should relate in some way to the ocean, for the dominant sound in Sydney is that of the sea; always there are the siren of some ship arriving or departing, the tooting of the horns of the tugboats assisting in these efforts, and the impatient sounding of the klaxon aboard the ferries. The raucous call of sea gulls mingles with the rumble of a train crossing the bridge, and both echo across the water. Freighters' winches can be heard day and night as they unload cargoes from the ends of the earth to deposit them in the miles of warehouses along the water or as they load the wealth of Australia to be shipped overseas in payment for the imports.

We had lunch at David Jones's Piccadilly, and that evening we tried pizza from a small Italian restaurant. In driving about the city exploring, we discovered that there are ethnic pockets where you can find almost any kind of food, and any level of financial living. On the North Shore there has been some attempt to preserve the bush that developers have plowed under elsewhere; there is contemporary architecture, which seems to be the hallmark of the "environmentally concerned" rich, and on back streets you see gardens featuring blue gums, golden wattle, and coral trees. In Lindfield, Killara, Pymble, and Wahroonga live the solid types with solid gardens. Down in Paddington are the artists and writers—and would-be artists and would-be writers—and the Bohemians who aspire to be arty or poetic; I have seen the same crowd in Los Angeles, Tucson, and New Orleans—poets with no music in their souls and artists blind to the beauty of disciplined art.

Between the extremes of Lindfield-Wahroonga to the north and Paddington in downtown is a huge city of people living an hour or even a two-hour bus ride from work, for it seems to be the dream of every Australian to have his own house and garden. This is easy to condemn because of the urban sprawl that results, but it certainly creates a higher incentive than the thought of having one's own apartment with 2,000 neighbors within arm's length.

That evening we were watching a local television production, the "$25,000 Great Temptation." This thriller originates in Sydney and is a quiz show much like "Sale of the Century," a TV epic that has gone off the air at home. The three contestants, one of them the big winner from the day before, are asked questions, getting five dollars or so for a correct answer. Periodically the three are allowed to buy some item for a ridiculously low sum—a washing machine for only nineteen dollars. I noticed, however, that the prizes here were astonishingly poor by American standards. This show, which is syndicated across the country, believed something worth twenty dollars or so a good prize.

A British import on TV that struck Richard and me as very funny was "On the Busses." However, Nancy thought it "nasty." I must admit it was far more adult than anything on American television.

The following day I spent mostly researching at the library of the University of New South Wales while Laura and the children shopped in the downtown area. During my lunch hour they joined me in Hyde Park, and we strolled about to admire the Anzac Monument and the gardens. To me this area seemed much prettier than Central Park in New York City, and to us there was no threat of being mugged.

That evening I learned from talking with Laura that people in Sydney apparently are complaining about the height of the AMP building and other skyscrapers in downtown Sydney, such as the Centrepoint Tower, which is under construction where Her Majesty's Arcade once stood. Apparently some of the people here do not want tall buildings, stating a preference for the old sandstone buildings once erected by convict labor and by the laboring free settlers. I guess it is human nature to complain about change, just as I know that someday in the not too distant future there will be editorials in the local papers praising with the best superlatives the skyscrapers of Sydney, just as editorial writers already praise the buildings in New York City, Chicago, and Los Angeles.

Somehow Sydney seems to me simultaneously like San Francisco and New York City. It has a charm and grace and an air of being connected intimately with the ocean that I associate with San Francisco, but it also has that air of importance, of "something happening," that I associate with New York City. The city coat-of-arms shows a bustling sailor, a guileless native, and has the motto, "I take but I surrender." That does not make a lot of sense. The city has a population of 2,700,000 or 3,000,000, depending on what source you read.

Again the following day I spent my time at the university doing research while Laura and the children explored the wonders of this city. After finishing up that afternoon, I went down to the Australian-American Club to talk with any Americans I might find. Actually this foray netted little that was not a repetition of what I had heard in Melbourne and Perth. One man I met, whose accent was so unmistakable I would have known without his telling me he was from New York, said, "I left the city because the level of crime there had become intolerable. I was afraid to work late because I had to walk to a parking garage to get my car, and I feared I would be mugged doing that. A fellow whose office was just two floors below mine was killed by a mugger in that garage one evening, and I knew I had to get out."

How could I tell him that the level of serious crime in Sydney was not appreciably smaller than that of New York City? Or that I had heard the Mafia was operating in Sydney and Melbourne? And why did he leave one big city to move to another, with similar problems? I could not answer those questions then—or now.

That evening, reading the paper, I was confronted with another curious aspect of the Australian character. They apparently have that British love of animals that passes all understanding (although they do not extend this love to the kangaroo, which is being slaughtered rapidly, or to the sheep, which they love to eat in the form of mutton). A judge somewhere in the country, in passing sentence on two murderers, said that the designation *human* ill-fitted them, that "the description *obscene animals* would be more apt." This statement, when repeated in the press, triggered several irate letters to the editor from animal lovers who stated that only humans were obscene and that the judge had insulted animals.

The next morning we drove through King's Cross as well as St. Kilda, but both were quiet on this Sunday. In fact, every Australian city seems almost totally dead on the Sabbath. So we decided to visit Taronga Zoo Park, for this would enable us to see both harbor and zoo. In order to get to the zoo, we had to go down to Circular Quay and catch the ferry out to the zoo. This cost $1.50 for adults and less for the children, and was worth every cent. At this excellent establishment for animals we saw the platypus; he looked as impossible in the flesh as he does in pictures.

The news of the day, however, was that the nurses' strike had been ended. They had been given pay raises of thirty-five to sixty percent depending on skill and years of service. For example, an RN (registered nurse) would get thirty-five percent more pay, raising her to $139.40 per week, while the first-year trainee was to receive $75.00 per week, a raise of sixty percent. Also, the postal workers, who had been on a slowdown strike, were to receive an additional $16.00 per week.

Where was the famed arbitration process of Australia? It disappeared with galloping inflation, and the Australian workers were striking just as regularly as their brethren overseas. Dr. Frank Crean, the federal treasurer, was openly stating that inflation had come to the nation because businessmen were "flabby." He said Australian business had "lost the initiative it sometimes claims" and that "there is a great deal of inefficiency within it." Without mentioning that the government itself might have been partly to blame for inflation, Dr. Crean stated that business "has had things too easy for too long, and is unable to accommodate itself to competition and to challenge."

My first thought was to dismiss Dr. Crean as a politician with less brainpower than courage—for I have never heard an American politician with the courage to say so bluntly that businessmen are not competitive. However, I remembered a conversation with an American two days previously in which we had been discussing local business and industry and the future of Australia. "See this suit," this American said to me, pointing to his clothes. "This is wool. Australian wool. However, I lost most of my belief in Australia's future when I discovered that this Australian wool is shipped to Taiwan for weaving into cloth and sewing into suits, then sent back to this nation. It tells you something about how little initiative there is here and how high the cost of labor is here."

Perhaps Dr. Crean has a glimmering of some higher truth. But how I wish he might examine the government itself to see about its efficiency. How I wish some American official would do the same at home.

During the next three days I continued to do research work at the library of the university while Laura and the children continued to explore and tour. However, they found it very difficult to find souvenirs, for there was really very little that was truly "Australian." Uniformly for sale everywhere were stuffed koala bears and stuffed kangaroos, even stuffed platypuses, all made from kangaroo hide. This made me wonder what they did with the rest of the kangaroos after the hides were ripped off. Then someone told me—they use the meat to make dog food, which is shipped to the United States. "Perhaps this is why some of your dogs may seem a bit jumpy, what?" the fellow informed me. I suspect this must be some Australian chestnut of considerable age, but still the fellow laughed heartily.

All the souvenir shops sell "aboriginal things": boomerangs, wooden spears, and assorted items. However, only Nancy wanted a stuffed animal (she has a collection of stuffed animals and purchased a koala, while we secretly purchased a stuffed platypus to give her on her next birthday as a surprise). Richard eventually settled for an Australian Rules football, which is similar in shape to an American football, but the ends are more rounded than our own. It was of quality leather and cost only six dollars.

We still needed to get something for ourselves and for a neighbor in Stillwater who was watching our house and collecting our mail. At last for her we settled on a wooden kangaroo on a stand; this was made of some kind of wood that was beautiful, and the workmanship was excellent. For ourselves, we decided to wait, hoping something better would turn up, for we could not settle on a bark painting, the only other typical souvenir item. These bark paintings are just what the name implies: pictures composed of different types of tree bark glued to some type of backing.

During this time I noticed in the newspaper an item that did not reassure me, and that I managed to keep Laura from seeing. It stated that food being exported from Australia was subject to rigid testing for purity; this, no doubt, was to ensure that these markets continued in the future. But food bound for the domestic market was not subject to inspection. As the reporter phrased it, "There is nothing beyond the basic honesty of the average manufacturer to prevent foodstuff reaching the market with microbiological contamination." Laura was just getting over her illness, and I did not want her to think too much about every bite that went into her mouth.

Another story in the paper amused me greatly. It concerned a performance of *Macbeth* at the Opera House for a group of high school students. Apparently Australians, even high school students, make known their feelings even more forcefully than do Americans, for these students threw fruit peelings, laughed at the actors, and coughed so loudly that they drowned out the words. I guess these youngsters appreciate Shakespeare about as much as do Americans of a similar age. I still remember how I suffered when I was in high school and had to read several of these plays. However, I and my fellow students were not as outspoken as were these students.

And Al Grassby, the ex-minister of immigration defeated in the last election, was still preaching about the need to end racism. He had stated that ninety-eight percent of all Australians wanted to end the white-only immigration policy, but that the other two percent generated "an influence totally out of proportion to their numbers." His view was that the country needed education that will make racism unacceptable. I really believe he did not know the public very well here. I recalled the story, told with great relish in Australia, about how Australian immigration officials keep out the undesirables. Australian law states that anyone seeking immigration must pass a literacy test, but it does not specify any one language; this is left to the immigration officials to decide. Thus when an Englishwoman of shrewish temperament asked to move to Australia, she was given her literacy test in Italian. Other nondesirable immigrants are treated in similar fashion; some are even given the literacy test in Gaelic, the ancient language of Ireland. Here is a case of government bureaucrats frustrating the ill-advised plans of the politicians.

One day at lunch I went out of the university library and walked in the Royal Botanic Gardens and then went on down to the Domain. This is where soapbox oratory is allowed. It was quiet that day—to my disappointment, for I had hoped to see this system working. All I heard was some teacher saying that the teachers should be given a twenty percent pay raise and $500 more a year in starting salaries.

Other stories in the newspapers, almost all of which made me think I was still in the United States, concerned industrial violence and a widespread fear of the thugs employed by the building trade unions to gain their ends. Other Australians were griping about "junk mail." And the recent floods, said a government official, would cause the price of onions and potatoes to rise 21.5 percent.

The newspapers here treated the impending visit of Frank Sinatra like that of British royalty. Pictures in the newspaper showed the jet that "Old Blue Eyes" would use, his dressing room, the Rolls Royce he would ride around in, and everything else connected with his visit. Apparently this American singer was quite popular. In Perth we had seen notices of contests wherein the winners were to get roundtrip air fare to Melbourne and two tickets to Sinatra's show there.

The morning we were to leave Sydney to drive to Canberra, the newspapers and television news were full of Sinatra's problem of the evening before. According to what we read and heard, the singer had quarreled with reporters, while his bodyguards roughed up some photographers who got too close. Sinatra then commented that reporters were "bums" and that one lady reporter was nothing but a "$1.50 hooker." Union leaders responded by demanding that Sinatra apologize or else they intended to picket his shows. Sinatra reacted to this threat by calling off his Australian tour —five shows that would guarantee him $650,000 (or almost $1,000,000 in American money). However, when the singer went to board his private airplane, he found that members of the Council of Trade Unions (about like our AFL-CIO) were sticking together and that he could not get his jet fueled. So he returned to his hotel suite, only to discover that union members would not bring food or drink up to him there. This in a country where Sinatra was extremely popular, which shows just how powerful the unions are in Australia.

Despite the intense heat of this incident, we managed to tear ourselves away and drive out highways 31 and 23 toward Canberra 190 miles away. This took us through an area known as the Southern Highlands, mostly over the Hume Highway (Australians have a habit of naming their major highways). This region reminded all four of us mainly of Pennsylvania, for the rolling hills were not really mountains. As we moved down this road, I became convinced that Australian drivers are among the world's worst, a conclusion I did not reach because I had to drive on the wrong side of the road. These people move past you at dizzy speeds while going up hills and around curves, moving with a reckless abandon that explains why they have one of the highest accident rates and death tolls in the world.

About 110 miles out of Sydney we came to the Wombeyan Caves, but at the last moment decided against entering. The establishment did not look too promising; besides, we had seen Carlsbad Caverns in New Mexico only the spring before, and this did not indicate anything new.

Actually I should say that this was 176 kilometers out of Sydney, for on July 1 Australia went metric. All the distance and speed signs are now given in kilometers rather than miles (but the British Petroleum road map of New South Wales, which cost me a quarter, still gave distances in miles). Apparently the changeover caused some problems, for I saw advertisements everywhere stating that information folders about the new system could be had free at local post offices. It was a real shock to me to see signs stating that the speed limit was 100—in kilometers, not miles. Richard and Nancy had the new math with its forced learning of the metric system, and they were not disturbed by this at all. But Laura and I had to translate everything slowly from kilometers into real distances and miles.

Later when we commented in Canberra that this country through which we had driven, the Southern Highlands, was not as mountainous as we had expected, we were told that the real mountains were to the southwest of Canberra. That would be the Snowy Range, over which we had flown more than a month ago en route to Tasmania.

Arriving in Canberra, we checked into our motel, ate our dinner, and listened to the "tellie" (as they sometimes called TV) to get the latest on the Sinatra hassle. However, we did not learn the outcome until the following morning when we found that Sinatra would give his performances after all. He finally stated that he "regrets" the incident. He never really apologized, but his lawyer and the union men did work out some settlement that pleased everyone.

The *Canberra Times* was the most "international" newspaper we had seen in Australia. By that I mean that more space was given over to international events than in any other newspaper in the country. Even Watergate, which seemed to be ignored for the most part elsewhere, was chronicled in some detail almost daily here. In local news that day the *Times* reported that the prime minister, Mr. Whitlam, had asked labor unions to practice wage restraint in this time of inflation. But the union leaders replied in terms that George Meany had used in response to President Nixon's similar request, telling the prime minister almost explicitly where he could go. The unions, both right and left, refused to ask for any less than they could get.

Laura and the children spent their first day here touring art galleries and museums rather than looking at the city, for the second day would be Saturday and I could join them in touring. My first day I spent working at the National University, still searching for similarities between the American West and the Australian experience in the Outback. My only comment about this place is that bureaucrats apparently are the same the world over.

The next day, Saturday, we toured Canberra. This is a planned city and really very lovely. The population is either 160,000 or 170,000 (we saw both figures cited). In trying to find some city in America or Canada with which to compare it, I am at a loss, for the town is new; it was created to be the capital, and much of the city is given over to governmental buildings of one kind or another. In short, it looks in part like Washington, D.C., but without the slums and the sprawl. The designers of the ACT (Australian Capital Territory) tried to avoid the mistakes made by Americans. Therefore, they do not sell land in the capital territory; rather they lease it for a set period of time, using the income thus generated to finance the federal building while retaining some control over the type of construction done here.

There are no billboards in this city, no utilities above ground, no slums, no factories, no used-car lots, and almost no litter. And most of the trees in the city were imported from the Northern Hemisphere, so Canberra does not really look Australian. In fact, I would sum up our impressions by saying that it does not look like any country or any other city.

The city planners estimate that the city will reach 300,000 residents by 1980, and they are planning ahead for this figure. Moreover, they claim that 1,000,000 visitors a year come here. I can believe this because every other person we met seemed to be connected with tourism in one way or another, and the other fifty percent worked for the government.

These civil servants did not work on Saturday or Sunday—heaven forbid—and so we found the town deserted. Therefore, we drove out to Red Hill, a viewpoint from which we could see the city entire: government buildings and monuments and even Lake Burley Griffin (named for the American architect who won the worldwide competition to design this city). Lake Burley Griffin is a man-made lake and serves as a reflecting pool for the monuments and government buildings surrounding it.

The following day, Sunday, we visited Parliament House but did not go inside (these buildings were closed to visitors on Sunday). We also toured the Botanic Gardens, the Australian War Memorial, and the Carillon (which had an advertised fifty-three bells that rang out—and deafened anyone nearby). While there we saw the Captain Cook water jets in Lake Burley Griffin; these shoot water 140 meters into the air and, we were told, put six tons of water into the air at any time these are running. Finally we took the lake cruise. With blue sky above and clear water below, the reflections were spectacular. However, it was too cold really to enjoy ourselves. The climate here is about like what we know in Oklahoma, for this is too far inland to be warmed by ocean breezes.

Canberra's freeways run in circles around the city. We followed these out to see the "new cities" being created in the capital territory: Woden-Weston, which opened in 1962; Belconnen, which opened in 1966; and Tuggeranong, just opening this year. Another of these, Gunghaling, is to open in 1976. These satellite towns are to keep Canberra from getting too large. They are little more than bedroom communities with a few service businesses and shopping centers, but are built in attractive fashion. However, our opinion was that we would not want to live in any of them; they seemed just a bit antiseptic. And they were too new to have any character. However, Queanbeyan, a small town just outside the capital territory, did have character; there you could see billboards and utility poles—even slot machines.

On Monday morning, as the government offices opened, there was a mad traffic rush in Canberra. And this afternoon at quitting time there was another. In between, however, very little was moving on the streets. Again I spent the day at the Australian National University, which has a famed center for social studies. I had to check in and show my credentials from my university at home—and was roundly fussed at for not writing in advance to establish myself as a bona fide scholar. This university is not open to the public; it runs a conducted tour, but you cannot just walk in and look around. Here I found many of the materials I wanted. Laura and the children spent the day shopping and touring.

One interesting facet of Australia's character presented itself to me as I read the book-review section of the local newspaper: an astonishingly large number of books are written and published in and about this country, more than would seem likely about a nation of only 13,000,000 people. I guess Australia is similar to Texas in this respect: the people here buy—and perhaps even read—books about their past.

And I see in the newspaper where Australia is going to begin testing cigarettes for tar and nicotine and will publish the results for the public. This will begin just as soon as a machine for this purpose arrives from the United States, a nation that has been testing its cigarettes since 1967. However, I think that these tests have not appreciably cut the amount of smoking in the United States—which doubtless will be the case in Australia. I suppose it will not be long before the Australian government bans cigarette commercials from television and radio. There will be screams about censorship, for it seems almost everyone here smokes heavily. I have not smoked now for nearly two months, but somehow it is comforting to hear the Marlboro commercials. I would hate to see these end.

The next day I again spent at the National University, while Laura and the children shopped, looked at houses, and visited various grocery stores. She found food prices rising here even more than at home. The following prices are given in Australian money (the American cost can be had by adding half again the amount shown): beef was sixty-five cents a pound for a hind quarter, forty-six cents a pound for a half; chicken and turkey were expensive at fifty-nine cents a pound. Other grocery prices compared almost exactly with the prices at home, which would make them quite expensive.

The recent floods, coming late in the fall, hurt Australia's harvest and drove prices up. Moreover, Australians were worrying about the spread of fruit flies, another factor pushing up prices. I remember that at the Sydney and Melbourne airports we were stopped at inspection stations and asked about any fruit we might be carrying; this was an attempt to halt the spread of these fruit flies. And the newspapers kept noting this effort and encouraging everyone to support it.

I suppose our curiosity got the best of us, but we decided that afternoon to fly out to see Ayers Rock and Alice Springs. "The Alice," as people refer to Alice Springs, is the only real town for a thousand miles in almost any direction and sits almost exactly in the center of the continent. We knew that there would be little to see there. However, we chose this, which is seen by almost all tourists who really "do" Australia, rather than go to see one of the opal mines. Australia produces about ninety-five percent of the world's supply of opals, but we opted to skip that and see something of the real Outback.

Thus the following morning, our arrangements made, we turned in our car and flew to Alice Springs, a flight that proved long—and hungry. We had to go first to Melbourne and then to Alice Springs, and did not have time to grab something to eat at Melbourne's airport. Arriving at the Alice, we found it pleasant after the weather we had experienced at Sydney and Canberra; these had been too rainy and cold. In the center of the continent, however, we found it cold in the evening but pleasant during the day. We were told that we had arrived at the best time of year; in the summer it is hot, and the flies here reportedly bite in a most unpleasant way.

Alice Springs looked like some movie set used and then abandoned by John Wayne: false fronts on the buildings, which all seem to prefer a "frontier" look. I was tempted to look to see if they were made of plastic. However, Richard and Nancy were fascinated by this town, which does have some wandering aborigines as well as places that teach how to throw a boomerang. I was curious to learn something more about that fellow from Vienna who intends to train camels and use them for tourist safaris, but no one in town seemed to know much about this.

The Outback is supposed to be empty, and I am certain that for hundreds of miles it is. However, you would never know it by looking around this town. Anywhere you looked there seemed to be a couple of busloads of tourists. We were told that this was a popular stop on tours for Americans; they were rushed in and out again, never really catching their breaths. Several times we were asked if we were part of some tour. When we answered negatively, the questioner seemed surprised.

The country around the town, we learned, is dusty during

the dry season of the year and soggy during the "wet," which is about two months of the year. And it is relatively free of pollution (except tourist pollution). Just looking at this region would drive some land developer from New Mexico or Arizona or Colorado crazy. All one of these people would have to do is bulldoze a few streets and roads, get a photographer skilled at the use of purple adjectives, and place advertisements for "ranchos for retirement or investment."

Here in our motel for the evening I saw an advertisement for Rabbit Flat Motel, which is out to the northwest of here in the Tanami Desert—and that must really be the middle of nowhere (or as some of the Spanish officers once called Arizona, "*El fin del mundo*"—"The end of the world"). This place features two-bed tents with meals in a tin shed and water from a bore (well). The price for bed and board at the Rabbit Flat Motel is $A12.25 per day, while bed only goes for $A4.90. But this is the only place for many miles where a bed can be rented, and I imagine the owner is doing all right. Some American kids who want to be their own boss and who want fresh air might think of coming over and giving this fellow competition.

The following morning we left Alice Springs at 7:30, catching a bus from our motel one hour before our flight out to Ayers Rock. The airline is Connair, and it flies a Convair 580 (the same equipment used by Frontier Airlines at home to serve Stillwater). It took us an hour and twenty minutes to reach our destination; on the way we passed over the Finke River, which has water in it once a year, and the Macdonnell Ranges, a spectacular chain of mountains jutting up from the desert. The rest of the countryside was bleak beyond description. If ever there is an atomic war, I suspect the world will look like this stretch of Australia after the big bombs go off. At last we landed very near the base of Ayers Rock.

We were met by a bus that took us to the Inland Motel— and, by golly, the place is appropriately named, for it is a long distance inland. We were told by our host aboard the bus that we were going to the motel for tea time, but in reality I suspect it was to sell us souvenirs. Afterward—and we resisted the temptation to purchase the souvenirs, although we did pay an arm and a leg for tea and sweets—we were driven around the base of this rock. I must admit the rock is spectacular; even Richard and Nancy, who had asked why on earth we were flying all this distance just to see some rock, were visibly impressed. The thing is five and one-half miles around at the base (the road around it is seven miles), and we stopped from time to time to visit caves where aborigines had painted their drawings on the wall; these looked like the work of some four-year-old. Our guide told us that the rock is 1,148 feet high, and it looked it.

Afterward we were driven back to the motel for lunch, one I could not recommend to any gourmet. Afterward we had two hours of free time in which we could look at aboriginal paintings for sale, at the caves, or use to climb to the top of the western end of this big rock; anywhere else it was impossible to climb, for it was too steep. Richard and Nancy did go part of the way up, but Laura and I preferred to get our impressions of it just standing there and looking up. This done, the bus took us back to the airstrip where we again boarded the Connair flight to return to Alice Springs at 5:30 P.M. For this trip we paid $A59 for adults for the 210-mile flight each way and for the bus service.

As we left Alice Springs that evening on a Trans-Australian Airlines flight back to Canberra, I was not sorry to go. The trinkets and junk for sale at Alice Springs had reminded me of the "genuine Indian artifacts" made by the Hong Kong tribe of Indians which are for sale throughout the American Southwest; most of this stuff also was manufactured in Hong Kong. The rest of it was made by genuine aborigines, but only after some Australian businessman had shown them what to do. Very little of it was genuine native artifacts. And all of it seemed terribly overpriced. I suspect that as Australians are made to feel yet more guilty about the way their natives have been treated, the price will go even higher, just as Indian artifacts have in the United States. The price seems to be correlated directly to the guilt level of the country.

We arrived back in Canberra at 9:30 that evening after losing half an hour going east. Australia has three time zones: the eastern zone; the central zone, which is half an hour behind the eastern zone; and the western zone, which is an hour and a half behind the central zone. We were so tired that we picked up our Holden, drove to the motel, and went to bed.

The following morning we left Canberra behind us, glancing back to see the public buildings and public monuments fade into the distance. We drove north to the town of Yass, northwest to Cootamundra, then turned northeast onto Highway 24. This stretch of country was very lonely, bordering the Outback, if it was not the real Outback itself. This still was grazed by sheep, however. We had the road totally to ourselves most of the time, and I found it difficult to stay on the left side of the road. Unconsciously I would begin to edge to the right side of the road to drive, then would jerk myself back to the left side. Occasionally a truck would come roaring down the highway; the teamsters here were as lordly as those back home.

As we drove I had time to ask Laura about the housing that she had looked at in Canberra, for we had not had the time to discuss this at any length before. She said that homes in Canberra were more international in design and architecture than anything else we had seen in Australia. This might be due to the number of foreigners and diplomats in the place, but she suspected that the variety came really because the town was new and the architects wanted to try a lot of new approaches. She had found housing there to be quite expensive: 2,600 square feet, four bedrooms for $A58,000. This one featured built-in "robes" (closets) and central heating, but it had no air-conditioning. And from what we heard, it does get hot in Canberra in the summer. Moreover, the down payment was about twenty-five percent.

Laura asked about the attitude of the professors at the Australian National University. I had not attempted to talk to any of those in history, but from my conversations at random with others there I found them to be as "ivory tower" for the most part as American professors; a wide gap separated them from the working people to whom we had talked. One American serving as a visiting professor, but who had some sense, gave the best comparison. He said the professors at the National University thought of themselves much like Harvard men, while those at the University of New South Wales thought of themselves as Yalies. The rest of those he had met, he said, were all right.

As we drove toward our destination for the night, Bathurst, we found the countryside getting bleaker and bleaker until the area looked much like some of the roughest parts of Nevada or Utah. There were vast stations (ranches) here, along with occasional kangaroos. Looking at the little towns we had passed through, we could understand why there were advertisements seeking teachers who would agree to go to the Northern Territory (or to Papua, New Guinea). If it was difficult to get teachers to come out to these little towns, it must be almost impossible to get anyone except Americans to go into the remote areas of the Northern Territory. We saw only a part of that from the air as we flew into Alice Springs and out to Ayers Rock, and it was barren and bleak.

Arriving at last at Bathurst, we were happy to turn on the heater in our room, for it was sufficiently cold to tell us that we were in the middle of the Australian winter. Just as we passed the reception desk in the motel on our way into the restaurant, an ambulance came wailing by, and I saw our host looking out intently. When I inquired about what was happening, he told me that the ambulance had been out to a remote area and was returning with a patient. In talking about this with the motel owner, I learned something about New South Wales that surprised me. The state is divided into fifty-six ambulance districts that are operated by the state. These are financed like insurance: each family that signs up pays $15.00, while a single person pays only $7.50. For this the state provides professional ambulance service for no additional charge (nonmembers needing an ambulance are charged $40.00 for the first sixteen kilometers and $1.00 per kilometer thereafter; needless to say, almost all residents of New South Wales sign up).

The next day we completed our drive, returning to Sydney through the Blue Mountains. This is quiet country, in places seeming very remote and beautiful, much like our Blue Ridge Mountains. Because these mountains are so lovely, however, people have flooded into the area to build weekend and vacation—and even permanent—homes. I stopped at one of these developments to talk for a while. And in a town we encountered some people very opposed to this type of development; their arguments sounded exactly like those of our Sierra Club people.

Here is the story the way I pieced it together: the environmentalists say that this stretch of the Blue Mountains is "teetering on the edge of environmental catastrophe," that the creeks are full of garbage and refuse and effluence and thus are unfit for drinking or swimming, that the vegetation has been damaged by the dumping of chemicals and rubbish, and that the Great Western Highway, since it was opened, has brought cars—and smog—into the area. These environmentalists have only one answer: a complete halt to all building, and they want the government to buy back many of the homes already built in order to bulldoze them and return the area to nature. They figure the cost of what they feel should be done is $A96,000,000.

The developers quite naturally claim that progress cannot be halted, and they want to go right on building in the area. They claim that this part of the Blue Mountains will grow from its present population of 40,000 to an eventual 275,000, and even more.

Construction on such a scale, say the environmentalists, will bring the destruction of historic buildings and of aboriginal treasures, as well as increase the risk of fire in the region. How familiar all this sounds! It reminds me of the fight going on between the same two groups over the development of the Lake Tahoe region on the Nevada-California border.

Some of the mileage and distance signs along the Great Western Highway had been changed to metric figures, but others had not, because of the heavy snow and floods experienced this year. Therefore, as we drove along we would see one sign that said "Speed 100" (in kilometers, of course), and then the next sign would proclaim "Speed 65" (in miles). This was confusing. However, on this stretch of road we saw no state police cars, so I guess it made no difference what speed we traveled.

Arriving at last in Sydney, we found the evening paper full of ads recommending that the reader should buy land and building sites on the beaches or in the mountains as a hedge against inflation. These were similar to our own ads recommending the purchase of land in Colorado, Arizona, or Florida. About all these things show is that speculators raise the price of land, and that some fools apparently buy it.

On Sunday we rested and then went to the horse races at Randwick here in Sydney. To our surprise we passed a McDonald's hamburger place as we drove out. Naturally Richard and Nancy wanted to eat there, and we did. I learned by asking that there were seven of these establishments in Sydney and three in Melbourne, and that many more would be built shortly in both cities. And still more were planned for the other capital cities. "We'll soon have more of our outlets here than does Colonel Sanders," the American manager told me proudly.

The food was not exactly like that served at McDonald's at home, at least not the way I remember it. Here they served hamburgers and chips but they also featured fish and chips along with fried chicken. "We have to sell what the people here seem to want," the manager told me with a shrug of his shoulders. But our luck was better at McDonald's than it was at the race track. Some of those horses on which we wagered at least fifty cents are still running, no doubt.

We had decided to go to Brisbane on the evening train today, but the day's newspaper almost changed our minds. According to the reports printed in the paper, Brisbane was experiencing a flu epidemic of such proportions that one-sixth of all the doctors were sick. And the same applied in Melbourne; in fact, doctors were needed so desperately in Melbourne that two weeks ago, when we were in town, there had been ads in the Sydney newspapers saying that doctors could earn three hundred dollars in a single day in Melbourne. A reporter from a Sydney newspaper checked out this report and wrote that the doctor would have to work an eighteen-hour day to earn that much. Despite this report, however, we decided to continue our journey. I already had suffered the flu, and no one else in the family had caught it from me; therefore, we reasoned, they would not likely catch it from someone else. That evening we turned in our car and boarded the *Brisbane Limited,* again to travel by rail.

VII.
The Northeast

We went down to the main railway terminal in Sydney to purchase tickets for the *Brisbane Limited,* the overnight train running up the coast from Sydney to the town for which it is named. This railway terminal was bright and relatively new—and had almost no personality. The terminal in Adelaide looked like a railway terminal; this one looked like some library, although it did have a clock that resembles Big Ben. We picked up the tickets we had reserved for the train leaving that evening and, with the caution born of some years of traveling, I inquired of the clerk about dinner on the train that night.

"No worry," he replied. "Dinner is served on the train."

Alas, we believed him and did not use the hour we had remaining to get something to eat. Instead we shopped for souvenirs until at 6:30 we boarded for the fifteen-hour run up the coast. Soon afterward Richard and Nancy were clamoring to be fed, a sentiment with which Laura and I concurred. We arrived at the "dinner" to be told, however, that no hot food was served, only toast, tea, and "railway pies." While we were discussing this menu, three Australian men came by and looked at the menu. I asked one of these men what a "railway pie" might be. He informed me that they were somewhat like the meat pies served in Adelaide and were usually very bad. "Don't eat them, mate," was the advice of one of the other Australian gentlemen. We heeded this advice and dined that evening on toast and tea.

Sleeping on this train proved easier than it had on the run across to Perth for some strange reason. The following morning we had yet more toast and tea for breakfast. In the breakfast car that morning an older Australian fellow was complaining loudly over his toast and tea that during World War II he had been fed better on a troop train running from Sydney to Brisbane than he was dining on the *Brisbane Limited* in 1974.

The morning paper, which somehow did find its way aboard this train, mentioned that a "supertrain" was being built at the South Australian Government's Railway Workshop. One of the prototype models had been completed at a cost of $A18,000,000, and would be sent around the nation for display, and propaganda. By 1976, according to this article, supertrains would be in service all over the country and would lure thousands of people back to train travel. The supertrain was to be faster, safer, more comfortable, and less noisy than present trains. They even supposedly would have less vibration. My hope, as I read the article, was that the supertrain might have a diner that served more than tea and toast for breakfast.

Perhaps it would be better than the incinerator in Sydney, which, the paper noted, everyone was laughing at. This incinerator cost $A5,200,000 to construct and went into service just thirteen months ago (June 1973). Now it was malfunctioning to the extent that the clean-air people from the government asserted the thing was giving off eleven times more air pollution than the level allowed under the Clean

Air Act. There was talk that it would be shut down—thus exemplifying what government action usually accomplishes.

At the railroad station in Brisbane we picked up our car, another Holden (all the Avis cars we had used so far wore a sign on the back window saying "Dunk Island"; that is one of the islands of the Great Barrier Reef, but no doubt its only function on these cars was to identify them to Avis). With a newly purchased map of Queensland, which also had an inset of downtown Brisbane, we navigated our way to the Crest International Hotel, where we had breakfast as quickly as possible. There in the restaurant was a classical gathering of "old boys." These were men in their sixties and seventies, all wearing blue jackets and white trousers, all with gray hair and gray moustaches (and some with gray wives). They looked as if they had just come in from the playing fields of Eton. No doubt, they were having some type of convention.

From the window of our room in the hotel we could look out on the top of city hall. This edifice had the appearance from the street of being Roman in architecture; from our vantage point, however, we could see that to the sides of the copper dome were flat tin roofs on the wings of the building. Earlier in the Sheraton Hotel in Perth we had noted that four- and five-story apartment buildings, which we could see from our room, had tin roofs. Obviously it never snowed in these cities, and the rainfall was scant; therefore, they must think it wasteful to spend money roofing that part of the building not normally seen. However, it did look peculiar.

Walking downtown that morning to do some shopping, we had yet another example of the pervasiveness of American culture. In the David Jones Department Store, we were upstairs in the Piccadilly when Nancy pointed to one of the kiddie rides and began laughing. This was one of those bucking-horse things that cost a penny to ride. Richard caught on and began laughing before Laura and I finally saw the point. On the side was a sign saying "Ride Trigger."

And here, as elsewhere in Australian cities, we noticed something else: no matter what time of day you were downtown, the sidewalks and streets were very, very crowded. It made me wonder who, if anyone, was working. Moreover, when you purchased something, the clerks were never in a hurry. They checked and double-checked their figures, counting very slowly and methodically—and then counted again. They absolutely refused to hurry, and they seemed never to get upset about anything.

Moreover, in walking about this city we noticed that the people of Brisbane seemed sloppier than other Australians. Perhaps this was because the city and the state of Queensland are tropical, and rot begins quickly in the tropics. Also here in Brisbane we saw our first slums as we drove around, houses that had not been kept up and that rivaled some of the sorry parts of American cities. Elsewhere we had seen old houses, but these had been painted and clean. Not so in Brisbane.

As we walked around downtown, Laura commented that not only were the streets of Australian cities always full, but also the bars were always filled. I looked and decided that she was right, a point that confirmed what we already had observed: that most Australians were serious about their drinking. This realization made me understand why some people wanted to found temperance societies—and these were still quite active in Australia; we saw their signs and their buildings in all the major cities.

That evening in our hotel restaurant, we met an American doing business in the city, and to him I confided my observation that few Australians seemed to want to work hard. "You're right," he responded. "They don't. The only people in this country who really do any work are the farmers and ranchers. That's because they're the only ones who have any real incentive to work. If they work hard, they make more money. But in the factories, if someone works hard he makes all his 'mates' hate him, and the shop steward will have a private talk with him about slowing down. I've been here almost four years, and thank God I'm about to go home. I thought American workers were bad until I got over here. These people live only for their holiday time."

The word *holiday*, I remembered, originally meant "holy day." Thus it was most appropriate that Australians called their vacation a holiday. To the typical Australian whom we met and read about, his four weeks off each year and his long weekends were indeed "holy." This businessman agreed with my thought. "The Aussies," he concluded on this subject, "are going to go the way of England if they don't get more interested in working. Right now the country pays its overseas bills only because it can export foodstuff and mineral commodities. Without these it would be lost."

On another topic this American had yet another insight to offer. "I've noticed," he said, "that Canadians traveling here hate it if they're taken for Americans. Well, Australians who are traveling hate to be taken for British."

This fellow gave me the names of some Americans living in Rockhampton with whom I could visit to get opinions about Australians, and these we filed away for use.

The next morning we loaded our car to head north. As we drove out of town we noticed that Brisbane, like Perth, had many new buildings under construction. The skyline would change, but not as swiftly as Perth's, we concluded. Yet Brisbane did have a distinct identity; we particularly were fascinated with the harbor area along the Brisbane River; here we could see oceangoing vessels loading and unloading.

Our goal that first day of driving north from Brisbane was Maryborough, a distance of 275 kilometers (or 172 miles, according to my mathematics). Once out of the city we began to see the older homes that once must have been standard in Queensland: wooden structures sitting up on high stilts with garages attached and with bananas, papayas, and frangipani growing in the yard.

This was a land of pineapples and bananas, citrus orchards, even of plantations of slim papaya trees. Much of the way I was trying to decide if this looked more like Florida or

Hawaii. Everywhere there were caravan (trailer) parks, motels, souvenir shops, and things for rent. The Bruce Highway (Highway 1) was not good, but not bad; it was two-lane and paved, going out to the ocean and back inland, weaving back and forth. Sometimes we had to slow down because of hills and curves, but always the drive was pretty. This was the region the tourist people liked to call the Sunshine Coast.

One unusual feature along this route was the Glasshouse Mountains. These, we were told at lunch, were named by Captain James Cook himself on his great voyage of discovery. The mountains were ten squat peaks thrusting straight up from the level plains; Cook thought they resembled the glass-blowing furnaces near his hometown in England. Our host at lunch also told us that this was a good region for quiet vacations. "Those seeking a jumping holiday go to the Gold Coast," he said, "while those with families tend to come here to the Sunshine Coast."

At Nambour, just north of the Glasshouse Mountains, we were in the midst of cane fields like those of Hawaii when we noted a signpost pointing the way up to the mountain plateau where Australia's only coffee and ginger were grown. Appealing as this sounded, we continued north, going through Gympie (where Queensland's first gold was discovered eleven decades ago) and arriving at last at Maryborough, a booming town astride the Mary River. Because of the river, coastal ships were built right in the middle of the town. This region, according to local information, produced about one-sixth of Australia's timber and sugar, one-fourth of the nation's pigs and dairy products, one-third of the corn, and three-quarters of Queensland's huge peanut crop. We found the food excellent and the motel accommodations reasonable in Maryborough, which could be moved to the west coast of Florida and no one would notice anything strange.

The next morning we set out on a more formidable drive: four hundred kilometers to Rockhampton. Most of this was inland, although occasionally from some high place we could see the ocean in the distance. This was sugarcane country, and also rum, so we learned. I thought of Fiji when I saw the little narrow-gauge railroad cars and tracks. These were used to haul the cane from the fields to the mills, and every little town—and some places in between—had sugar mills.

The next major city north of Maryborough was Bundaberg, but to go there meant we had to leave the Bruce Highway and drive almost fifty kilometers to the northeast (and, of course, fifty kilometers back). Therefore, we bypassed this city, famous in all of Australia for the quality of the rum produced there. We were told that distilling began there ninety years ago when artesian wells proved a source of water so soft that even yet it has to be hardened artificially before it tastes right to the palate. Also, at Bundaberg the surf ends; for 1,200 miles to the north there is no surf as the Great Barrier Reef prevents any waves from crashing into the beach.

We did leave the road at one point. This was to drive out to Gladstone, twenty-one kilometers to the east and on the beach. This is another ocean port. Until about 1960 Gladstone was dwindling quietly away to nothing, another city going to rot in the tropical sun. Its only source of income was a meatpacking plant that loaded an occasional ship, plus a few tourists that came here to go out to Heron Island, which has excellent coral reefs. Now coal is shipped out from here to Japan; just a few miles inland they discovered huge deposits of a type of coal needed to make quality steel. And at Gladstone there now is a huge alumina plant; the bauxite used in this plant is mined at Weipa (far to the north just on the west side of Cape York Peninsula), and brought 1,500 miles by sea in ships to Gladstone, and is here smelted into aluminum. We toyed briefly with the idea of taking the helicopter ride out to Heron Island, for none of us had ever ridden in a helicopter; however, the price of the ride caused us to remember that we needed to push on to Rockhampton.

North of Gladstone the country flattened out somewhat, and there were more sheep and cattle grazing and less sugarcane. Some people have called Queensland "Australia's Texas," and we can see why. This is a big state with a great deal of different geography. But it is far more tropical than most of Texas, at least along the coast. All the little towns have palm trees in the streets as well as that tropical look about them. And all the men, it seemed, were wearing shorts and knee-socks rather than long trousers.

Just before we entered Rockhampton we crossed the Tropic of Capricorn. This was marked by an aluminum spire, but not a very impressive one. The city itself was a far greater monument. Along Quay Street we saw the massive stone fronts on wool-brokerage houses—stores selling things needed out on the sheep stations—and office buildings; even the Customs House was of the same stone front and massive pillars. The streets were unusually wide, and the people walking along them seemed never in a hurry. From what we could tell, the affluence here derived from the cattle and sheep of the interior, although nearby Mt. Morgan produced copper and even gold (and had since 1862). "Rich as Mt. Morgan" once was a phrase used to describe anyone or anything wealthy.

The newspaper that evening mentioned several strikes that were getting a lot of attention. Especially important to the local people was a strike by marine engineers; needed supplies, said the story, would be allowed to sail (several of the little coastal towns still depended on ships to get what they needed). Postmen had been given a thirty-six-and-three-quarter-hour week, and therefore were ending their slowdown strike nationwide; they thereby became the first government employees to get less than a forty-hour week, but where they have pioneered the others doubtless soon will follow. And stewards on Qantas Airlines had settled their strike in favor of a four-day, forty-eight-hour week with pay raises of thirty-one to sixty-six dollars per week.

Australia is far more heavily unionized than the United States. My reading of the implications of this is that Australia is far more likely to go the way of England than of the United States: a slow decline in productivity and living standards until it becomes just another banana republic. The only reasons it has kept growing so far have been: (1) foreign investment, which keeps coming in at a record clip, according to governmental records; (2) the new mineral discoveries, particularly in the north and northwest; (3) continued agricultural productivity, which will increase as technology provides access to yet more water; and (4) the arrival of New Australians, who apparently are still willing to work to earn some of the things they want.

In fact, I think if Australia is to continue to have a high standard of living, it must develop its water resources, thereby making productive the vast amounts of land it has. Australia is as large as the continental United States, yet very little of the land is under cultivation. Perhaps Australia's real hope for the future is desalting ocean water, piping it inland, and opening the fertile soil to cultivation.

And the country needs this now. There is renewed talk of devaluing the Australian dollar because labor costs have made the nation's goods uncompetitive overseas. Such a devaluation would be a real break for new immigrants (and for American tourists), but now there is only talk. Naturally it will not happen until after we go home.

The Rockhampton paper also had a front-page story about a shark attack on a Texas family in the Gulf of Mexico. My bet is that the story was hardly mentioned at home; however, the people living along this coast are very shark-conscious. That night someone in the motel dining room, learning we were Americans, told us that Cornel Wilde, the Hollywood actor and producer, was here recently filming some underwater scenes of sharks for one of his movies because this was the best place in the world to see sharks.

The following morning we caught the Trans-Australian Airlines flight out to Great Keppel Island. TAA made this run in a little putt-putt plane that covered the thirty miles in twenty minutes. We then spent the day walking on the beach and riding a glass-bottom boat. This was the south end of the Great Barrier Reef, and here you saw coral and tropical fish in such profusion and such riot of color that the trip was most worthwhile. In fact, we were so enthralled that we kicked ourselves for not making a reservation at the resort hotel here on the island, but we had left our suitcases and our rent-a-car waiting for us back at the Rockhampton Airport. Therefore, we had to return on the late afternoon flight.

For those who really want to get away from it all, however, the State Forestry Office in Rockhampton has a bargain. You can buy a permit there that allows you to camp out on any of the uninhabited islands in the reef—and there apparently are hundreds of these islands; you are warned to pick one with a dependable water supply or else to take your own water. To get to the island of your choice, you make arrangements with some charter boat owner to drop you off and pick you up later at some prearranged time. I think this would be more solitude than I or most Americans would want, however.

The newspapers that afternoon were full of talk about the coming of color television to Australia in the near future. Color TV sets would go on sale on August 1, a week away, and were expensive by American standards. The cheapest set would be one with a twenty-two-inch screen for $A650. And all you could see on it until March 1, 1975, would be a test pattern in color. The rest would still be in black and white.

Moreover, the newspaper reported that members of Parliament were talking about giving themselves another raise. They last voted themselves more money (52.6 percent) less than a year and a half ago (March 1973). But inflation had hit them also, and the members apparently wanted more. They have a permanent committee that periodically examines the pay rate of government officials and makes recommendations. At present MPs received $A18,600, the prime minister $A56,500, and cabinet members $A33,975. Of course, Parliament could vote down a recommended raise if members so desired, but I am sufficiently the cynic to doubt they would deny themselves this increase. The Australian system is not *that* different from the American system (indeed, I saw awhile back that a Liberal candidate in a state by-election reportedly found his telephone had been bugged).

All this land up here—and so far we had been driving along the thickly inhabited part—and yet the prices were similar to those in the United States. An advertisement in the Brisbane newspaper, which we got here, showed 640 acres of land in Queensland for sale at $A14,900. That seemed cheap enough, but another ad for just 160 acres listed a price of $A20,000. Prices apparently depended on location, rainfall, and fertility. The price of lots in Brisbane ranged from $A2,000 to $A10,000, also depending on location. New houses in that town could be had for as low as $A15,000. Apparently housing in Brisbane was about the same as in Perth, but lower than in Sydney and Melbourne. In the latter two cities the price of land had gone so high that townhouses and condominiums were being built faster than any other type of housing; and some of the condos (as they were called in Australia) were going high-rise, with many, many stories.

That evening in Rockhampton I did look up one of the Americans whose name had been given me, and he called the other man to come over. It seems that they were friends and got together often although there was considerable difference in their ages. One had moved to Australia just after World War II, during which he had married an Aussie; the other had come more recently. "We've had a good life here," said the fellow who had been stationed in Brisbane during World War II. "But fifteen years after I came here, that would be in 1961, I went home to visit relatives—and left just as fast as I could. I guess I've become more Australian than American, for I couldn't stand what had happened at home." He paused and reflected, "No, that's not true. I'm an American who has stayed an American of 1946. I look at the Americans I see on television and in the movies, and I read in the newspapers what they are saying, and I don't understand the Americans of the 1970s. They run down their own country. They are rich, but they seem to want to look as ugly as possible. According to them, there's nothing good about America. I don't like most of the Americans I meet now."

The other fellow, the younger one, echoed the same thought. "Five years after I moved here," he said, "I got homesick and started to go home. But I got as far as Hawaii and saw the freeways with their mad traffic, the big hotels, and the half-blistered, underdressed tourists, and I said, 'That's not for me.' I came back and took out citizenship papers here."

I commented that Australians played tourist also, to which both responded in similar vein: "Yes, they do. But they don't lose their dignity doing it. There is still a certain amount of gentility here."

The next morning we set off on a long drive that took us inland to the town of Miles. Most of this was through the Great Dividing Range, and in places we had to drive very slow. This for the most part was sheep country, although we did see some cattle; however, we were told that the cattle country was mainly to the northwest of this part of the state. We did not really get far enough inland to see the really arid country. However, we could tell that we were getting away from the land of heavy rainfall. Again, the land began to look like New Mexico or Wyoming once we got through the mountains.

In the little towns some distance inland, we began to see a few aborigines. They looked even blacker than Afro-Americans, and somehow were different; they appeared millions of years old. The federal government was beginning to provide these people with free legal aid, which I deem wrong, for it is a legal recognition that the aborigines are different from other Australians (who do not get free legal aid). You do not make people equal by setting them apart from everyone else. Moreover, this sets a pattern for bureaucratic paternalism, which is wrong.

Sometimes these natives were called "Abos," but this apparently was a derogatory term, much like *nigger* at home.

The aborigines have some preserves (reservations) set

aside for their own use and permanent home. Great Palm Island, just off the coast of Townsville in northern Queensland, is one such place. On this island are a few summer homes for bureaucratic officials, but most of it belongs to the natives. However, this island is a place of good beaches, a sunny and mild climate, good fishing, wooded hills, and lots of fresh water. In short, it is exactly the kind of place developers dream about for setting up a high-priced resort. So the government is maneuvering to take Great Palm Island away from the aborigines—for their own good, of course. The liberals here are in full cry against this move.

Another story told here is about how the aborigines worship the green ants at Gabo Djang (in northern Queensland). Well, an outfit named Queensland Mines, Ltd., has discovered that there is uranium ore of high quality under these anthills, and they want the land taken from the aborigines. The natives have refused to sell, for apparently they fear that disturbing their sacred ants will turn the insects into man-eating monsters.

All this reminds me of the Indian situation at home, at least as the Indian situation stood eight or ten years ago. All the bleeding hearts hereabouts have concluded that the aborigines are Nature's Noblemen, and that the white race in the past has been guilty of oppression and sundry misdeeds; therefore, the only way to atone for all this is in the future to give these people special treatment. Australia's liberals do not want to make the aborigines "take the white man's road." They feel the aborigines' culture is so special that it is worthy of imitation and preservation—yet they simultaneously believe the aborigines should have access to all the material goods the white civilization has produced. I wish a few of the bleeding hearts would go out and live with Nature's Noblemen for a time—I mean live as the natives are living now. They soon would sing a different tune about the glories of this kind of life.

I was told by several Australians that far to the north on the Cape York Peninsula, where there are aboriginal preserves as yet little explored, the aborigines will kill any white man they see. Perhaps we might ship a few dozen of the leading liberals up there to preach their message of aboriginal superiority.

At Miles we found a takeout food place that advertised American food, and we ate there because Richard and Nancy were hungry for a hamburger. This proved a disappointment. It is impossible to duplicate American cooking in Australia—or the cooking of any country in another (although Colonel Sanders manages to ruin chicken equally well everywhere). You cannot get the same result using the exact same recipe, for the ingredients differ from place to place. I recall when we moved from Arizona to Oklahoma and discovered that in our own kitchen Laura could not make Mexican food taste as it had in Arizona; although she bought the same ingredients in the grocery store, they were different in Oklahoma. The same holds in Australia; the hamburger is ground more coarsely, the bun is like French bread in texture, the catsup (or tomato sauce) tastes different, and even the mustard is not the same. So a hamburger made in Australia exactly as it is made in the United States tastes different! The ingredients just are not the same. In Tasmania everything picks up the flavor of the gum tree. The flavor of any region is unique, and it colors the taste of the food prepared there.

In Miles I heard there was an American teaching school, so I sought her out. Several times in the past, some of my students finishing a degree in history and searching for a place to teach had asked me about the possibility of jobs in Australia. I therefore was anxious to learn about this from someone with firsthand experience.

The young lady was from Tennessee, and could not tell me why she chose to come to Australia. After talking with her for a while, I concluded her motive was the same as that of a young man who joins the Marine Corps: adventure. "I saw a notice that teachers were needed over here," she said, "so I applied. My family was against it, but I wanted to travel before I marry and settle down, and this seemed an inexpensive way to see Australia."

In return for signing up for two years of teaching at any school assigned her in the state of Queensland, she received roundtrip transportation. Her salary would have been much lower, about $A1,800 lower, had she agreed to teach only in an urban school, but she chose to accept employment in any town in the state in return for the higher salary. Naturally she was placed in one of the more remote places. "They're paying even more, I hear, for teachers in the Northern Territory and in New Guinea," she said.

Her application had been processed not through the Australian consulate but through a professor at Cal State University in Hayward, California. "He handles Victoria, Tasmania, Western Australia, and Queensland," she explained. "Those teachers going into New South Wales get higher salaries than we do in Queensland," she had heard, "but the teachers for that state are recruited by an official of the New South Wales Education Department, and he works out of New York City."

"Was the process of selection difficult?" I wanted to know.

"Yes," she responded. "They tried every way possible to discourage me. I guess they wanted to make dead certain I would stay the full two years. I had to sign an agreement that I would repay my transportation costs over if I quit early. The process took three months, it involved a lot of paperwork, and I had to get recommendations about my scholarship, my teaching ability, my character, and even my morals. They really checked me out closely."

This paralleled what I had heard about the difficulties of getting a permanent visa or assisted immigration to become a citizen. For this, so I had heard, you needed to be white, under forty, and have some definite skill that Australia needs. If you were separated or divorced, you must produce the legal papers on this. And if you were trying to move there with underage children and were a single parent, you had to have all kinds of notarized statements showing that you had custody and that, if you were divorced, the other parent approved your taking them out of the country.

My next question to this young lady in Miles was about the differences she had found in Australian and American children. "The children here," she said, "are far more respectful of their elders. They obey me better. They don't question everything they're told to do, and they still want to please you. And because the girls and boys are separated in school, there are a lot fewer problems."

In our general discussion, several other factors emerged. The teachers of Australia are unionized, and the union is a strong factor protecting the teacher from administrators. Moreover, the teachers all follow state curriculum guides far more closely than we do in the United States. Everyone teaches the same thing in every grade at the same time. There is little room for innovation or change except in a governmentally approved way.

"What's your major problem this year?" I queried.

"You won't believe it because it is so foreign," she replied. "Here they have a Parents and Citizens Association, which is the equivalent of our Parents and Teachers Association. The PCA, as it is called, is federated nationally. Well, the local chapter, like the national federation, is angry about the cost of school uniforms which almost all Australian schoolchildren have to wear. The cost for these for both summer and winter has risen to about $A100, and the parents are in an uproar. That's $100 for just two uniforms, one for summer and one for winter. Naturally a lot of the children outgrow these before the end of the year. We had a manufacturer's representative in to talk to our PCA. He pointed out that often it is the school at fault. Each school chooses its own colors and then asks for expensive cloth and an intricate design. Thus these uniforms cannot be made on an assembly line; they have to be made by hand. This manufacturer said that if parents want cheaper uniforms they will have to demand that schools get together and standardize. Then the uniforms can be made on an assembly line. Here our school officials responded that they run a clothing pool where used uniforms are sold, and that this helps cut the costs. Boy, this has been a fight!"

At our motel restaurant that evening I got yet another view of this same situation when I fell to talking to some people from a town a hundred miles farther into the interior. Many of the young Americans who come over to teach, I learned, sign up to accept a teaching position in the back country because this promises more pay and because they think they want the rural life. They want to pioneer. Then they get over here, these city kids, and they discover that pioneering is lonely business and hard work. So they break their contract, call daddy, and ask for money to get home. Or, even worse, they stay and gripe for two years. Many Australian parents are unhappy, therefore, when they learn that their children are to be taught by an American. They want better screening of foreigners coming over to teach.

"These American youngsters are screened by professors who are liberal," this fellow told me. "And they are idealistic. And they send us liberal and idealistic young teachers. We don't need that. We want some practical people to do a practical job. Even worse, many of these youngsters who come over are strictly from the big city, and they get out to our community and just do not fit in." It seems, I would conclude, that Australian parents do not want young, idealistic, liberal, urban, and dissatisfied Americans teaching their children—and I cannot blame them.

The next morning there was a story in the newspaper about the Teachers' Federation of New South Wales (the labor union for teachers) wanting to blacklist all persons appointed to "senior positions" in colleges of advanced education if they came from outside the New South Wales teaching system. This would be a real change from union demands of the past. Today, thanks to the demands made by unions in years past, all academic jobs in Australia must be advertised nationally in all the capital city newspapers, and anyone can apply. This supposedly makes certain that merit is the basis of selection for university teaching positions. But now the unions in New South Wales want to keep these jobs for their own members, not have them given for silly reasons like merit. This might be understandable, but it is contrary to everything an educator is supposed to stand for.

That day we had our most beautiful drive yet. Returning to Brisbane, we came down the Warrego Highway through a region of wheatfields, then over the Dividing Range to the town of Toowoomba. In two months this city would have its Carnival of Flowers (it is called the Garden City), but we were too early for that. Boomerangs were manufactured nearby at the town of Mudgeeraba and sold all over Australia (stamped "Made in Queensland"). Richard, of course, bought one of them. So many of these things were like the "Indian" stuff at home: manufactured by people with no native blood in them, and then decorated with a few swipes of paint in some pattern supposedly aboriginal.

Back in Brisbane and in a good hotel, we had yet another good steak dinner. While the children watched TV, I read the evening newspaper. In this I learned that the American ambassador was under vicious attack by a Labour senator from Victoria. The senator asserted that the American ambassador was a hatchet man representing the American economic interests, which were bent on destroying democracy in Australia (and also the Philippines, according to the senator). The purpose of this plot was to keep Australia an economic dependency. The senator also charged that there was a huge CIA network operating in Australia—for what purpose he did not say, nor could I figure out. He concluded by asserting that the prime minister would agree with his assessment when all the "facts" were made known. I think the senator was trying to use the United States as a whipping boy for Australia's economic woes with inflation. And should the United States halt the importation of Australian beef, then the senator would be widely believed, for that would cause real economic dislocations.

The newspaper also noted that the Queensland Turf Club

of Brisbane was about to stage its second annual race wherein all the jockeys were female. That race in 1973 had attracted the largest amount of betting for the day, so they would repeat it again on August 31. In it would be a female jockey from North America, another from Europe, and ten from Australia. The purse for the winning horse would be $A10,000, a huge purse for Australian tracks, and the winning jockey would get an additional $A500 plus her share of the purse.

I mention this because any American thinking of moving to Australia to get away from the women's liberation movement will be disappointed. Women are on the move in Australia also. The fem-lib theme song, "I Am Woman," was the work of Helen Reddy, an Australian.

Finally, there were many letters to the editor complaining about foul-ups in computer billing by various companies in Australia, even one complaining about a company threatening him for payment of goods he had not ordered. In 1975 Australians will get their own credit card. The nine major banks have banded together to form a corporation that will issue the "Bankcard," which will be mailed out—unsolicited—to some 1,000,000 of the banks' customers. Naturally this has brought on talk about the use to which the confidential information gathered on cardholders will be used and who will have access to it. Civil libertarians have to be vigilant everywhere!

The next morning we drove down the Gold Coast. Now that term has a ring to it to set any tourist's heart beating a little faster. Technically the Gold Coast is a thirty-kilometer strip from Southport down to Coolangatta, all of which is just to the south of Brisbane. This stretch has sandy beaches and good climate, but because of high seas this year the waves had washed away some of the sand, and this hurt the resort owners. Also, the winter weather this year had been severe, and they were having a bad year. A southerly was blowing today, and we were cold when we got out of the car.

Driving down this road, I concluded that the entire thing

was one big plastic swindle, all made to look as much as possible like southern Florida. Even the names were American: Key West Motel, Montana Motel, Cuba Flats, Florida Court, Caribbean . . . , New Orleans. . . . And there was a Marineland here with trained seals and dolphins, along with old automobile museums and a long string of hotels and motels and nightclubs and restaurants and "attractions" designed to separate you from your money and make you think you are having a good time. When I looked at all this and began to get angry, I wondered whether it was I who was out of step. It seems there are many people who think they have not had a good vacation unless they come to some plastic spot like this, where the prices are too high and where too many people are crowded together.

Also along this road were many caravan (trailer) parks, each advertising that it had "barbecue units available." Barbecuing is really big in Australia; these people like their meat turned into charcoal on these things.

But the electrical system is different. Australia is on a 240-volt system (as opposed to our 110-volt system), so American appliances do not work here without a converter. Most of the major hotels in the capital cities have built-in converters so that American visitors can operate their shavers, but elsewhere you will ruin them if you plug them in. And the television system is British, not American, so your set would not work even with an electrical converter.

We stayed the night at Coolangatta, at the south end of the Gold Coast—also the cheapest and quietest part. It is birdwatching country, we were told. Actually we were in Tweed's Head, New South Wales, which is just across the state line from Coolangatta, Queensland. This still is resort country, however, for the state of New South Wales has developed this region in the hope of luring vacationers to it. At the motels and hotels along this strip, there were two sets of prices: the usual high ones, and then yet higher ones for the period of December 21 to January 31, the Christmas holidays, and for school holiday periods early in May and in August.

The next morning, our last in Australia, we drove back up the road to Brisbane, turned our car in to Avis at the airport, and boarded a flight to Sydney. As we lifted off and banked to head south, we had one last good view of Brisbane and its harbor. To dock in town, ships come the five or six miles from the coast up the Brisbane River, but ten miles farther upriver, the Brisbane is not big enough to float a rowboat. On this flight I glanced at a newspaper and saw that a group of financiers wanted to locate a major gambling casino on the Gold Coast and was seeking the necessary licenses. There was one big gambling casino in Hobart, and another was to be built in Launceston; still another group was trying to put a casino on King Island in Bass Strait. Yet this group wanted one here. But then I could see no reason why anyone would oppose it. Australia has legal gambling on horse races, and there is offtrack betting on these. Why not casinos?

Finally, I saw in this paper a strong editorial against American hippies. It seems the local citizens do not want hippies allowed into the country for fear they will be a bad influence on local kids, as well as promote illegal drug use. And should one of these American hippies take a job, said the writer of the editorial, he will be doing an Australian out of the job. So keep them at home, America, was the message.

At the Sydney airport, we took the bus across to the international terminal, and there we shopped for some last-minute souvenir of Australia. There, walking through the airport, I saw one man's anonymous comment to the liberals who would change the nation; above an elevator sign proclaiming "Staff Only," someone had scratched in bold letters "Whites Only."

At the souvenir shop, I glanced at the newspaper and saw a headline stating that Leyland (a British automobile assembly company) was laying off a thousand workers because of inflation and fewer car sales than anticipated. One angry worker had told the reporter that many of those laid off were driving Japanese cars and that "preference for foreign products contributes to our own unemployment." Well, all of us, Americans and Australians, may end up working for the Japanese. This reminded me of a currently common saying in Australia: "Once we worked for the British. Now we work for the Japanese. But at least in the old days we could talk to our owners in our own language." I remembered Hawaii and how the Japanese were taking over there.

The same newspaper had another front-page story about inflation: grocery prices had risen three percent in June and were expected to rise a similar amount in July. Finally, I saw in that paper a story that seemed to sum up how British the Australians are. Lawn bowling, from what I could gather, is something of a cross between bowling as we know it and shuffleboard, and can be—and is—played by people far along in years. According to the secretary of the Royal Victorian Lawn Bowling Association, the rulebook states, "If a club member dies on the green, then all games are cancelled for the rest of the day. Of course, if he's a visitor, you don't stop the games unless there are special circumstances."

With this in mind, we walked around to the Pan American boarding gate to wait for our plane. There in the lounge I looked around at the passengers waiting to board to see if I could tell which were Americans and which were not. And I could see a difference—a cleanliness, a substantiality to the cut of their clothes, a look of quality, and of modernity of fashion. Especially was this true of the shoes; American shoes looked solid and expensive compared with those of other countries. The Australians waiting to board looked similar, but there was a subtle difference that could be observed (and I tested my observation by listening as each of the waiting passengers checked through customs; there I could hear what nationality they were). Finally there was a look about Americans, a look that said they owned the earth.

It was raining as we boarded our flight, just as it had been raining when we arrived. Apparently this would be one of the rainiest years in Australian history. If this proved to be part of some permanent changing pattern to the world's weather (as, for example, the drought in Africa), then much change would come to Australia.

Once our flight was in the air, the stewardesses served us Coca-Cola and complimentary dry-roasted almonds. I looked at the package in which the almonds came and found that the ingredients listed were: destrin, hydrolyzed vegetable protein, yeast, monosodium glutamate, and flavoring. We were indeed going home when simple almonds had to have all this gunk added—but they did taste good.

Fiji passed in the middle of the night, made unhappy only by the spraying of the plane with DDT to kill off any insects we might have brought with us. My thought was that it was the Australian bugs that would suffer, not the Fijian insects. Then we came to Hawaii, where we had to go through customs and change planes. Several more hours and we were in Los Angeles to spend the night breathing smog in a Sheraton Inn, eating hamburgers, and drinking milk shakes. Freeway noises and jet lag combined to keep us awake well into the night—watching the same silly movie we had seen on television in Adelaide late one night. We were home.

VIII.

The Australian Alternative in Retrospect

ALMOST THREE MONTHS later, as we looked back at the summer we had spent in Australia, we found the memory of that experience a happy one. We did enjoy Australia and the Australian people.

In many respects Australia is like the United States of some thirty years ago: air-conditioning and the plastic age have not yet fully arrived there. Central heating still consists of an electric-coil heater mounted on the wall, and trolley cars still run in the major cities. And the pace of life is slower with the problems of an atomic world heard speaking with a muffled voice. There is not that sense of perpetual crisis that we know in the United States thanks to television newscasts that bring us tomorrow's worries at 10:00 each evening to disturb our sleep.

In short, Australia is a place to get away from it all, for the newspapers and TV commentators do concentrate almost exclusively on internal affairs. People wear out their clothes, take care of their automobiles, and do not allow their houses to go to ruin. Natural resources are conserved because the people, by and large, have not reached that stage of affluence that allows planned obsolescence to become a way of life.

Yet our problems are their problems: crime is increasing there at the same alarming rate as here; even organized crime has come to the Land Down Under; pollution is noticeable in the big cities, especially smog; inflation is galloping at a pace even greater than we know; interest rates are skyrocketing; the price of housing has moved to a point where the average man no longer can afford a new home; politicians promise just as wildly while lining their own pockets; taxes are higher than here; and gasoline, though we had no problem purchasing it, is even more expensive than in the United States (when we were there, 56.7¢ to 60.7¢ a gallon, but the cost in American money would be half again as much).

And they seem to catch all the bad aspects of whatever is faddish in the United States. For example, just as we were leaving I noticed in a paper that there was a move afoot in the schools of New South Wales to increase the amount of science and math taken by children. Called the Vaughn Scheme, this new plan also provided that almost no one would be failed. Some frustrated Australian wrote to the editor, "A system which will not fail the fool is a fool's system." That is as well put as ever I have heard anything phrased. Still the plan will be made operational; all will be passed in the public schools, while reading, writing, social studies, and the arts will be downgraded. No doubt the result in Australia will be the same as here: mediocrity will run rampant, and soon many of those getting high school diplomas will be unable to read them. But when this plan goes into effect, the educationists of Australia will point with pride and say, "See how we've improved the system; no one fails any more."

But it is not these things that disturb the thoughtful person considering a permanent move to Australia. Rather, it is the small things—like the wretched coffee we were served everywhere. Of course, this was partially offset by the high quality of the tea we were served; and tea time does seem better than our own coffee break because of the large number of sweets served with it. But after drinking coffee for many years, it is difficult to adjust to the change.

The food we were served was almost uniformly excellent, especially the steak, and usually it was priced very moderately. Most of this was immediately recognizable to Americans: steaks, roasts, ham, chicken, and fish. But there were some cultural shocks: spaghetti on toast and stewed tomatoes for breakfast. But in every restaurant we were reminded that we were foreigners because water was not served. Nor did they drink milk in any quantity; rather, they seemed to prefer their dairy products in the form of butter, for pats of this were served on almost everything we ordered.

The newspapers generally were of tabloid size and sold for seven cents. In every major city there were several newspapers, not just one or two. These generally carried only local news plus something about the royal family of England. While we were there, the queen's brother, the duke of Gloucester, died. The front page of every newspaper headlined the story, telling how much the deceased loved Australia and carrying yet another long story about some pimply faced youth who had succeeded to the title (he was described as a sensitive, artistic young man).

The cars we rented were different. Oh, a Holden is just a Chevrolet Nova, while a Ford Falcon looks just like its American counterpart. But all have the steering wheel on the wrong side, and the drivers do not know as yet to drive on the righthand side of the road. Every time we went out I was reminded by this perverse Australian habit that I was in some foreign land. And the speedometers, as well as road signs, now are in metric—which produces a shock for Americans. When the captain comes on the intercom in airplanes and says that the temperature in Sydney is five degrees, or the weather man on television predicts that the high for tomorrow will be fifteen degrees, your eyes open wide.

No, it is these small things that are discordant to the American ear, to say nothing of the slight differences in the shadings of words themselves. Therefore, I concluded that I would not want to live in Australia. They have the same problems we have without the same high standard of living—and the country is filled with foreigners. I was glad to get home.

In the notebook I kept during the visit, I notice that I answered the questions I wrote there in advance of the trip. "Would I want to live there permanently?" carries the answer "Not particularly."

"Would I want to go over again for a year?" My answer was "Possibly. It depends on where." I think I could live a year in Adelaide or Perth, but not Brisbane or Sydney or Melbourne. Tasmania was so different that I cannot really answer for that island.

"Did I enjoy it enough to visit it again?" The answer to this was an unqualified "Definitely."

Also in my notes I tried to analyze the different types of Americans whom we met that were living in the country. These fell into five categories: (1) big-city Americans who hated the city and moved—to settle in Melbourne or Sydney; (2) disappointed liberals and conservatives who had moved to Australia because of the deterioration they detected in the quality of life at home—and then became nonpolitical (those who did take some interest seemed just as unhappy in Australia as they had been at home, for politicians there are just as human as those here); (3) businessmen, usually still young, who went there to get rich, who saw opportunity and have seized it; (4) farmers and ranchers who were there for the same reason as the businessmen, and who likewise seemed to be doing well; and (5) the lunatic fringe who were trying to escape family or personal problems, but who took these with them inside their heads.

The reasons most often cited for moving were: (1) opportunity in a new country; (2) disappointment at home because of violence, drugs, racial problems (most of the conservatives cited racial problems as a reason for moving), and environment (and most of the liberals I met said they were looking for a better environment); (3) Australia promised to be a better place to raise a family; (4) a slower pace of life in Australia; and (5) a quest for a better quality of life (which each individual defines for himself).

My own reaction to all of this was that most of the people who moved to Australia could have had the same thing at home had they been willing to move to a smaller town or else just get off the economic treadmill. One does not have to move 9,000 miles to quit competing with the Joneses. Moreover, our observation was that most Americans had not found a heaven in Australia; rather, they had just changed the nature of their problems. Perhaps the best insight we had into the problem of immigration came when we were touring Hawaii and met that Australian couple thinking of moving to the United States—because they thought the tax laws here were more favorable than at home. All too often people conclude that a move somewhere else will solve all the problems that have accumulated in their lives. But that Australian couple at least recognized that the tax laws of their nation do not favor the accumulation of wealth—unless you take wealth with you. And if you have the wealth to take with you, then life anywhere can be pretty good.

In conclusion, however, I did find one reason for visiting Australia that I regard as valid: a vacation there is a good time to quit smoking. Perhaps if I organize a tour group of smokers looking to join the unhooked generation, I can get my way paid back down there. And, despite how happy we were to get home again, we do look forward to making another trip to Australia, not to escape anything, but merely to enjoy visiting a warm and friendly country. Just one thing: next time we intend to get our shots before we stop even briefly in Fiji.

The Faulks found that the Americans they met Down Under fell mostly into five broad categories: "(1) big-city Americans who hated the city and moved — to settle in Melbourne or Sydney; (2) disappointed liberals and conservatives who had moved to Australia because of the deterioration they detected in the quality of life at home—and then became nonpolitical (those who did take some interest seemed just as unhappy in Australia as they had been at home, for politicians there are just as human as those here); (3) businessmen, usually still young, who went there to get rich, who saw opportunity and have seized it; (4) farmers and ranchers who were there for the same reason as the businessmen, and who likewise seemed to be doing well; and (5) the lunatic fringe who were trying to escape family or personal problems, but who took these with them inside their heads."

Top, left to right: Richard, Nancy and Laura Faulk on the beach at the Australian Gold Coast.

Below: Odie Faulk is amused by a typical Hawaiian souvenir.

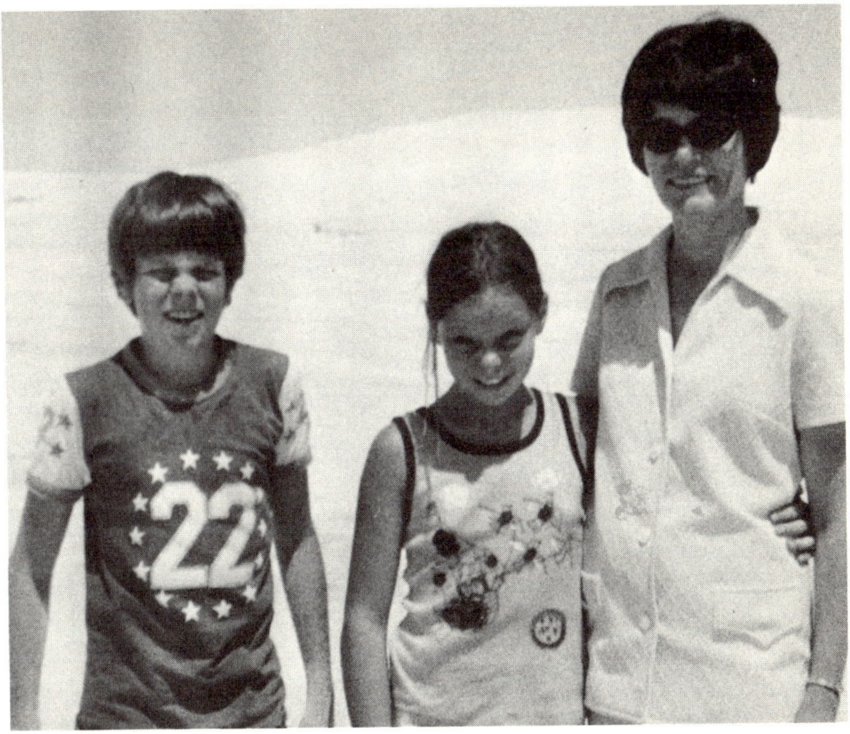
22

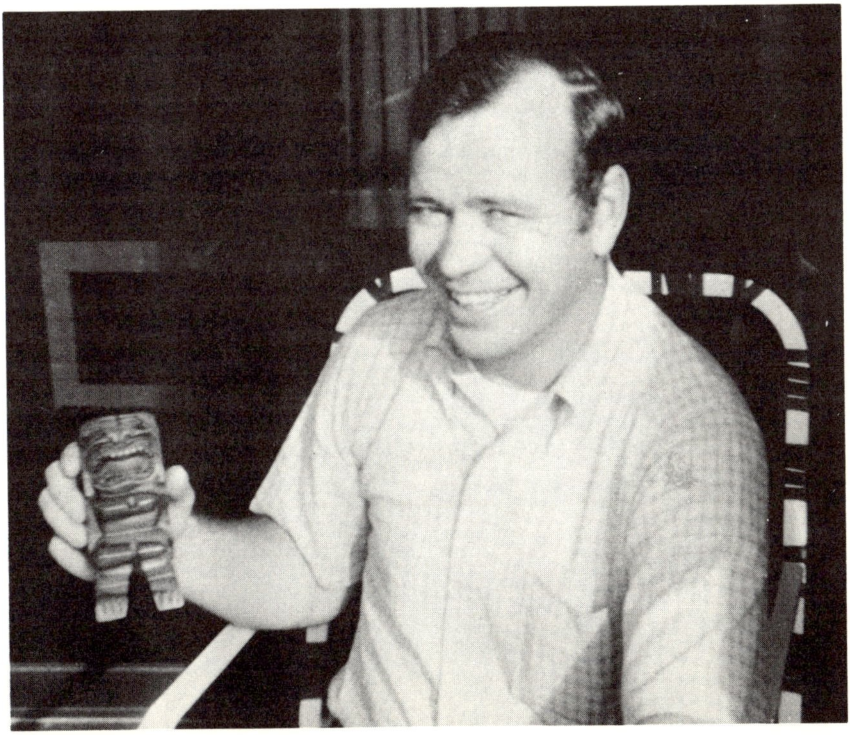